Invisible Poets

Anthology 1

FUNDRAISING IN AID OF

First published by
Wheelsong Books
United Kingdom

Cover photo © Amy Wheeler, 2024
Book design and layout © Steve Wheeler, 2024
First published in 2024

Print ISBN: 9-798-87760-714-9

Contents

—

—

9

Foreword

This book contains more than 350 poems. To be included, each had to be performed on *Live Poets Society*. Only the best poetry features on the show, which is broadcast live on the *Invisible Poets* Facebook group in the UK, the USA and South Africa. The hosts are all fairly savvy when it comes to poetry, but they also have eclectic tastes. As a result, the poetry in this anthology is diverse, with a huge variety of themes, styles and formats. There should be something for everyone inside these pages.

Your purchase of this anthology will not only benefit all the poets who are represented within these pages by gaining them a wider audience; it will also go a long way toward supporting children in crisis. Proceeds from the Amazon sales of this book will be donated to Save the Children — a worldwide relief fund that provides children in warzones and disaster areas with food, medicine, clothing, shelter — and eventually — education. It's a very worthy cause and we thank you for your valuable support.

Steve Wheeler
Poet and Founder
Invisible Poets and
Wheelsong Books

Standing Still at the Speed of Light
Joseph Gallagher

If I were a hummingbird perched still and quiet
On an upper myrtle branch in the summer heat,
And you were my mate alone in the whole heavens
Of sky above me, having parted yourself for me
From cedar top and honeysuckle stem the sea
Winds catching your wings lifting your body,
Hovering now in mid-air, floating far away
From jewel weed, thistle and bee balm.

And if I watched how you fell plummeting before me
And how you rose again and fell with such mastery
That I believed for a moment you were the sky,
And the colors of your coat—that feathered shining
Was just the physical revelation of the light's
Most perfect desire...

And if I saw your turning and swirling celebration
Of feathers whispered by wind, cutting the air,
This weaving, twisting, twirling vision of red petal
And nectar and the rush of your wing in its grand circle
Of arcing and splitting, created completely out of nothing
Just for me.

Then when you came down to me, I would call you my own
Spinning plume of ruby sage, my funnelling storm
Of sunlit cinnamon and pollen, my own breathless piece
Of scarlet sky and I would bless the base
Of each of your feathers and touch the tine of muscles
Binding your wings and taste the honey
In your crimson flare...
And I would take, and take you, and take you,
Deep into any nest you wanted.

Legacy
Neil Forsyth

Let the prose flow,
From your head to your toes,
Let verses lyrically
Suppress your woes.
Let stories be told,
Let your dreams unfold,
Let magic be practiced,
Let hearts be of gold.
Let words be your guide,
Let you speak them with pride.
Let your chapter be endless,
May you never be friendless,
Let your happiness show,
Let your families grow,
Let your legacy live long,
Let our futures be strong.

Wake Me Not
Gregory Richard Barden

oh, love …

do you still dream?
pray so, find me here
and haunt me —
stab me with those beautiful,
bloodless lies
I'll believe it all …
til waking

there —
I sit, toes in cold sand
wishing on a gulf as wide as mortality
Sol, bright as bright
but no warmth
only a brume of miracles
puffed away by the chill breath
of what's real
(and wild whispers, once yours)

yet, here —
I feel it all again … intensely
as if these lifetimes had not passed
as if your first smile 'hello'
had just found me speechless
brown-eyed blonde magic
turning me a child —
splitting me like a log
heart, no longer my own
as true as truth when
I'm in this fantasy's meandering
praying to slumber on

beg, these soft petals
of sleep's flower
do not shed for the thorns of
the waking world
where I cannot speak your name
or place my kiss upon your eyes
or drown their diurnal dark
oh, haunt me …

my love.

Her Last Goodbye

Marie Harris

Her last goodbye
Releasing doves into the sky
Carrying her forever love
And the question why

Why he had to be the one leaving
Creating an emptiness deep,
one she wanted to hide
A soul weary with the pain
And a need to keep her emotions
locked inside

With the winging of the doves
Wings carrying them toward heaven
Offering her heart a moment of peace
With a lifetime melody of love he gave,
without question

Lonely days ahead, stretching into years
With her heart taking momentary flight
Soaring with the doves into the blue
Until their journey was out of sight

A release of tears paving the way
As the doves flew effortlessly free
A healing sense of letting go
Knowing one day, together they would be

A breeze felt, gently caressing
A soft kiss upon her cheek
A heart-warming touch of goodbye
From a love, gone but waiting and
a promise of forever to keep

Untrained and Disassociated
Verse of beto

Untrained and disassociated
Intelligence do not make a
Civilization. In these dark ages of
The spirit, those who lust for a new
Creation have sought the new man and
May have found him — drugged by a
Flower. And he was seen in a
Violent storm that pounded money
Thru the should be world. He was
Crouching in the dark unkept corner
Of his world, waiting for a keeper
To make it right and feed him. He
Was bitter in the layers of
Nakedness that he had pulled over
Himself to become wanted, to become
Part, to become — and he was
Waiting when they saw him. They
Were terrified and they turned away,
And silently crept back into the
Crumbled ruins of their own corners.

The Gypsy
Charlene Phare

Trees deserted in golden sand
Swollen skies hover over land
Laminated lake, shimmers glow
The dunes remain from long ago

Lost in the desert all alone
The Gypsy in me loves to roam
As long as my compass points to north
I'll keep travelling back and forth
Back and forth, back and forth

Love to discover history
Peeling back world's mysteries
Learning about what transcends
Burning candles at both ends

Lost in the desert all alone
The Gypsy in me loves to roam
As long as my compass points to north
I'll keep travelling back and forth
Back and forth, back and forth

World is full of inspiration
Doesn't matter what location
Anywhere between the moon
And soft landings upon the dunes

Lost in the desert all alone
The Gypsy in me loves to roam
As long as my compass points to north
I'll keep travelling back and forth
Back and forth, back and forth

Take me to the dunes, where sands drift
Life's full of glory, a special gift
Keep my compass pointing north
Ignite my bones in earths warmth

Lost in the desert all alone
The Gypsy in me loves to roam
As long as my compass points to north
I'll keep travelling back and forth
Back and forth, back and forth

Portrait of the Artist as an Old Man
Terry Bridges

Knit me a pearl of wisdom into my heart,
A comforting scarf, you always wore one,
Scalloped round the neck, wind-torn.
I bought you a green gift, golden-studded
With shamrocks, on our Dublin escapade.
After strictly walkabouts for hours,
A half a pig sandwich in Neary's bar,
The huge ham crammed into soda-bread,
And thirst-quenching ale. That's what we did and said.
It was one customer's fiftieth birthday do.
Balloons, Guinness, the hard stuff the whole shebang.
There's no barman like an Irish wise-cracker,
Equally cool and competent at Trinity College,
Or shepherding recalcitrant cattle to market,
Or writing, or dealing with the over-fortified
With grace and gently persuasive humour,
Or being idle and celebrating at funerals.
Sing the praises of the Irish and Ireland.
May you never disappear into exile my love.
You are my rock, my genuine shamrock.
I wear your scarf as a banner of joy.

Desperate Hours
Karen Bessette

Such desperate hours now without love.
I watch the streetlights shine
from my window late at night.
Soon, the lonely ones appear,
lost silhouettes in the rain.
They look up at me slowly one by one
as if they know somehow we are the same.

Take Me with Your Breath

Lucille A LaRoche

I hear your gentle waves
Caressing the shores
Your ripples, echoes
A sweet melody
In synchrony

Like a breath
You soon exhale
A gentle sound
Like a summer breeze
You soon retreat
Much like humanity
You breathe rhythmically

You arrive and soon recede
In a timely fashion
In all seasons under
The Sun and the Moon

My Storm of Pain

Rafik Romdhani

I am the wood that dreams of mud.
I am a bleeding wound opposite to the wind,
approaching your soft hands to be cured.
There is fire above me and there is fire
beneath me, my sweetest love.
Above me there is your beautiful picture
drunk with nectar and birds' rapture.
But beneath, there is your heart, singing
to me and dancing with my storm of pain.

In the Midnight Garden's Gloom
James Eaton

In the midnight garden's gloom
Parabolic trees just loom
Long of shadow, deep of scent
I know not where the flowers went.

It was an autumn long ago
Where the Styx and Tiber flow
Intermingled falling leaves
Along a narrow pathway weaves.

We clasped hands at end of day
Then you were gone, so far away
Haunted now and forever more
I see the old cast iron shore.

The Liver birds are restless now
Green with age, they take a bow
My ship has sailed to God knows where
Tomorrow is the May Day fair.

Winter's Grasp Releasing
Neil Mason

the devil's weather is packing up
its wintery belongings and leaving town
carrying harshness in an icy suitcase,
labelled 'not needed here this time of year'
winters grasp releasing slowly but surely
a fresh season comes to visit
friendly buds leap into action
colours explode with vitality and promise
winters grasp releasing its hold on life
open hands shower the world with rich kindness
flowery bouquets grow inside loving gardens

Waves Of The Sea

Charles Lipanda Mahigwe

I am a poet with no pen and paper
Words ripple on lips like soft wind
Valiant voice rustles in me to speak
For the orphans whose blood flows
With the viscosity of the fluids

Our flag is dying for we failed
To protect our mother Congo
We brought war instead of peace
When will you stop grinding and crushing us?
We are spices in the mortar
How long will these bloodsheds
be streaming in the runnel?
We are refugees with no shelter

The rhythm of hymn is sung by our souls
For the guns have killed us in the wild refuge
When will these battered years end?
A wave of nostalgia ringing
Reflecting and appealing
When our dead parents were alive
Who would sleep on mat with no net?

'Cacia trees were vibrating to the beat of guns
We are vestiges of victims
And being pushed away like pebbles in the river
Walking in the penumbra
As stars dancing in auroras

We are transients
Poetry is aesthetic home
She protects us even during insomniac monsoon
We live in hyacinth
For it is where my father was reincarnated

I smell the scent of air
In the petunia of graves
For our bodies are rutted
When we all ululated
For being penurious
On the waves of the sea

Before
Rhiannon Owens

I walked here before when I was still naive
I walked here before, my heart sang, I believed...
I walked here before, this was my new start
I walked here before, I saw your face, you stole my heart...
I walked here before and I longed for your kiss
I walked and I walked - hoping you'd remember us...
(you'd remember this...)

Walked fingers crossed; Cupid's arrow did not miss
Walked on with a smile, because I was loved...
Walked on, walked tall as the sun shone above

Mother's Embrace
Michael Hislop

Clutched in Mother's embrace
Her skies, red ablaze
Impregnated our universe
With Prophecy's Child
Resounding in history
Human legends
Myth and lore

And Like Sands

James Martin

Our smiles are cracks in heaven's door...
cascading down....stifling malaise.
I've seen them many times before...
but alas, much fewer these days.

And now, as I twirl my smile wand
in orchestral, symphonic bliss....
I trust that I shall come upon
no lament in our final kiss.

For life has shone its lamp on me
through those darkened perilous nights....
transcending mediocrity
in far journeys to find the light.

Yet glancing back in retrospect
I notice you not far behind.
You make me proud to give respect....
as your pillars support mankind.

And so it goes through smiles and tears...
We soon pass through the hourglass...
unknown before our birthing years
and forgotten after we pass.

Weeping Orpheus!
Madhu Gangopadhyay

Darkness swept!
His wife was dead.
Orpheus of Thrace begged and wept;
To the pale moon!
As the frayed curtain of night wrapped him;
Biting emptiness engulfed!
Music robbed, his heart sobbed:
Calliope couldn't invoke a verse
For her grieving son;
Eurydice was gone!
The viper stung,
When in love's swing they swung!
Slithering pain!
Caustic melancholy,
The venom of separation spread.
What begot such fate?

Aristaeus's fatal chase!
The madly in love couple ran,
The wife fell on the poisonous snake!
To the organza moon
Orpheus beseeched for help!
On that ruinous night,
For his lovely wife
He bitterly cried!
The moon shed
Tears of grey light!
Charcoal vapours of despair
Envy is love's blight!

poems generated by artificial intelligence

Matt Elmore

words color artificial sugars on plastic cake
culminating in blank tastes AI poems make
never to really feel the abstract or surreal
only to cut and paste boil peel and steal

unable to substantiate relations humane
balance good evil common arcane
infernal mechanism translate every ism
incisions on derisions operating imprisoned

replicating emotions indebted to notions
capitalized prizes of sales promotions
purveyors of creation shallow reflect
mathematical programmers narrow concept

antithesis to soul of poets forever curious
for expression of perception set in experience
painting pictures constricted to digital lines
colorless meaningless devoid of esoteric minds

reconciling worth of touch hearing and sight
muting vivid voice of night and spirit alike
an existence bedevilled on unholy levels
raised by faith only to be buried with shovels

spitting out drivel purposefully superficial
pretentious perceptions simplified and uncivil
denied snuggles warm in lovely cuddles
stripping substance of lessons born of struggle

from flawed intelligence led by imperfect pleas
heartless words mock flesh and blood realities
to seek living wisdom from a breathless tutor
there is simply no divinity within a computer

A Dance in the Moonlight

Marie Harris

Under the moonlight glow
A dance of surrender
As her heart felt the pull
Of the moon's magic encounter

Her gown a diaphanous breeze
Softly falling around her ghostly pale
As she performed a lonely ballet
As the night wrapped her in a midnight veil

Within the silence, the music of her heart
Played an old familiar melody inside
Against her will she had to dance
Through the fall of memories, undenied

Enveloped as the night layered its dark
Under the moon's golden glow
A figure in a dance haunting
A solitary ballerina dancing in a softly ebbing slow

Under the spell the moon has cast
She is transported to yesterday
When the love attached to her soul
Was meant to last forever and a day

For her fate was a frivolous thing
Turning her world upside down
Leaving her a figure dancing in the moonlight
Searching for her partner that will never be found

A whispering breeze touches in a familiar caress
An echo of his voice so softly spoken
As her heart so vehemently wished
Today to be her yesterday,
when her heart remained unbroken

Our Dance
Joe Callanan

It's more than likely I'll step
on your feet during our dance
That why I've got my apology
prepared well in advance

If I step lightly on your toes
depending on how the music goes
First on your left then on the right
I'll ruin your high heels tonight

When you dance with me
I'll hold you close and tight
On our own or for all to see
Well dance all through the night

Renaissance
Neil Forsyth

A rebirth of the fire
That burned inside you,
Lighting the way
After those cruelties denied you.
A regrowth that grew,
From the tiniest spark,
That flickering candescence,
Emerged from the dark.
The losses you faced
As you tried to move on,
Those heartfelt memories
Of loved ones who've gone
You can never replace them,
Or would you want to,
Be it after the darkness
Life goes on for you.

I Want to Live Forever

Kirsty Howarth

I want to live forever
Can you hear me cry
I want to live forever
I don't want to die

In a world of darkness
Where I once stood in the sun
The lights have turned off
And from this I cannot run

I want to live forever
I refuse to face what's real
I want to live forever
Do you know the pain I feel

I feel like I'm suffocating
And drowning in despair
My heart is beating really fast
Does anybody really care

I want to live forever
Can you hear my screams
I want to live forever
As I still have my dreams

My head is spinning fast
Round and round it goes
My body's feeling numb
From my head down to my toes

I want to live forever
Take this thing away
I want to live forever
As in this world I want to stay

I'm going through the motions
And I'm in survival mode

—

I feel like I'm carrying
An extra heavy load

I need to survive the storm
And defeat for me is never
A warrior in battle
As I want to live forever

Long Fingers
Susan Ila Davis

Dawn awoke with tantalizing breeze
Long fingers stretched out in silent sadness
No secrets that your love had brought
madness
Gone, the warmth of your nearness to me
Caressing sheets, all my longing concealed
The dreams for us come taunting me again
Alight Truth, why I miss you in the end
I needed more than our skin could reveal
Night falls, the ticking clock rebelling sleep
No regrets, because your face was so sweet
I wanted you, long fingers on the breeze
No sleepy eyes were kissed in ecstasy
My soul is free, for a new love lingers
No longer the hostage in your fingers

Sea Star (Wishing)
Rhiannon Owens

A woman weeps gently into the sand
As her daughters splash in the sea,
A joyful little tableau
But there's a hole in their family,

Listlessly, she stares
As clouds gather on the horizon,
The air is turning chilly

—

Her girls she keeps her eyes upon,

They search for pretty shells
Their laughter tears at her heart,
So young, too young...
Don't they know everything's torn apart,

'Mummy' shouts one
'Mummy!'
Little legs pumping across the sand,
And she presses a star shape
Into her mother's hand,

Excitedly... 'When daddy had to leave us
I wished upon a star,
Look! That star has fallen to Earth
So daddy knows where we are!'

The starfish is dead and broken
And her other daughter begins to cry,
Holding up the broken piece
'Was daddy's angel hurt
When he fell from the sky?'

The woman's tears fall rapidly
How to ever explain,
How to cast away this dead 'star'
How to talk away the pain?

And then, a wriggle against her fingers,
The sea star begins to move
And her daughters shout in delight
As the broken bit does so too...

'It's Daddy... Daddy's watching us!'
Yes... watching from above,
They wished; he sent a sea star
To remind them of his love...

—

Dare to Reach

Jody Scott Kaplan

Dare to reach
You just might elevate
more than yourself
Some links need to be broken
Reach beyond the chains
Of preconception
Of same old
Of marketing flames
Hearing is more than volume
More of hearts engaging
Dare to see
The reaches
Just might be freedom
At last

Phantasmagoria

Safdar Bhatti

When that the twilight ascends,
Memories rise serenely
On the pupils, fearful ghosts,

Spectres in a hundred fold
Wearing the artful Venus
Sink and rise in dreaming eye
And the head, spuriously;

A teenager brilliance struts
Ambitious, ardent, eager
To attain the cliffy peaks

Hung far from his striving reach
Scolding in deriding jests

And yokel genius of slums;
Anglophile Sir Poetic
Dreams about life at Oxbridge
Quite like the genial Jude—

Poverty cries to the world
And the monkeys look, mocking

A slender, middle age man
Stumbling long at foolishness
Adheres to the restless beats
Of a mystic, wild vision
Passes ether and above
Floating in ecstatic joy

And the amateur poet
Lyrical in sighing lines
Pours his rhythmical drizzle
In a fondly naive dream,

Oozes out love, oozes out
Wanton desires of the flesh
Sings to various muses
Songs of languid appetite
Smouldering since the eons

This witching kaleidoscope
Continues its many shows
Until the bald, dozing man
Lifts his long languishing eyes
At the serene blush of dawn

Crimson Dawn
Rafik Romdhani

You can make believe
you are the god of knowledge,
the crimson dawn in the horizon
that shows up like infinity's edge.

You can make believe
that you represent the tiny cage
positioned amidst your ribs
and you expect the image of time
to be ruminating there like a sage
banned for life for his brooding mind.

You can make believe
that the entire world is in your hands
and you are the nucleus
where everything must die to live.

You can make believe
that the opportune moment has come,
pumping more air for you to breathe
while all else around you are dying
while you are the only one to continue to live.

You can make believe
you are the only crimson dawn in a horizon
muffled in thick blankets of grief.

Drops

Eric Aguilar

What is the secret of a tear
and where do you find its wisdom?
It is in the salt of the soul
from where the teardrops.
Cast into falling, should the lid
hold swell billowed and bulged,
let the eye see through and find
spiritual vision, for so have visions
come to the spirit who's been torn by grief.
By the seeping of tears, some have gone blind.
A lamenting madness ensues when
a heart is fully torn, twisted, and broken.
Wisdom is in the wash of the face,
from tears falling off crowns.
Perception is in the understanding, insight, and clarity
after the residue of the salt is chipped away.
The wisdom of a tear is that it drops because
it holds the weight of your sorrows.
Peace is the release of letting go.
But, the secret of a tear is that
it can spark a fire within you.

The Last of Us

Matt Cording

Only The best of us
would probably be the last of us
And the rest of us might be the best of us
But we'd have to pass a test of us
To see if we would be the last of us
I don't think I'd pass the test of us
But I really don't know about the rest of us
Would you be the last of us?
Me, I couldn't even run for a bus
Let alone be the best of the rest of the last of us

Wrestling with Emotions

Andy Allen

The bell rang
On the end of our love
When you landed from above;
An elbow drop to my heart.

You had
My heart in a half Nelson
And ignored my remonstrations
Then wriggled from my arms.

I knew
That something was amiss
Then I saw you and him kiss
A moonsault side slam.

How could
You tag him by the ring and
Put his ring on your finger
When I'd offered you my hand?

You hurt
Me with that back stab.
It was like a Boston crab
That shocked me to the spine.

But I came
Rebounding off the ropes,
My future held out hope
This was my washing line.

You didn't
Like me with someone new
It seems we suplexed you
And I heard you wail and howl.

You cried
Like I'd never seen before
In love's cruel mandible claw
And you threw in the towel.

Map
Suzanne Newman

My scars are a map of warzones where I've been,
Reminders of trials and the traumas I've seen,
They make me recall times of hardship and pain,
I have scars on my body and scars in my brain.

But I'm unashamed of my deep battle-scars,
For they all prove how God pulled me
through deadly harm,
I've felt the Grim Reaper loom up once or twice,
And have been unafraid, for I'm redeemed in Christ.

My scars are my medals to show God's great grace,
How He helped me withstand, kept me growing and braced,
And each twisted scar the Lord made and caressed,
And placed strength and love in them,
to leave me so blessed.

And if you join up all the lines of my scars,
You'll see they're a map, leading up a small path,
That lays past the Narrow Gate, heading for Glory,
For scars are the witness to my Christian story.

The Little Poem
George Valler

It's dawn that rolls the morning sky
And calls awake both you and I
The pillow talk, enough now said
Need now to step, walk from the bed
So claim awake the daylight hour
A moments take, to now devour
Night hides not, for all to soon
Dark now calls, now calls the moon

Glow
Gregory Richard Barden

a wink …

I got a wink —
and a tiny crook of a smile …
deep in the ink of her eyes,
the ocean, reflected with moonlight,
swept in staggered rhythm
to the scratchy shoreline,
looking like waves of thought,
(tho' I knew her thoughts were on me)
if only, I dreamed …
she reached out and pinched
a chunk of my cheek,
tenderly shook it as if I were
a naughty child,
let go, touching an index to my lips,
then lay slowly back
against the blanket-covered dunes …
a broader smile now,
one filled with coyness and
deliberate desire,
and then … a giggle …
"oh, sweet stuff!," she said,
"please … *please* don't waste that moon!"
I turned and looked up,
filling my soul with the bluesy Luna,
and breathing deep the warm, briny air,
then turned back to her …
"not a chance, my love …"

"…not a wink!"

My BFF
Patti Woosley

I can count on you to come around
and cheer me up when I'm feeling down.

Your crazy humor keeps me laughing strong
on days when everything
I do goes wrong.

There one thing I know
when each day is through,
you're my best friend forever,
and I can always count on you.

The Second Fall
Madhu Gangopadhyay

I saw the bougainvillea
Turn from pink to white.
Soon the green would drape
Mahogany hue;
And then the view
Would be painted anew!

Summer would flaunt
Its graceful charm
Scattering scent of jasmine.

The fall in February
In the Indian plains
Makes perfect rhyme

The earth is scripting
A midsummer sonnet.

—

Igniting Kiss

Emmelia M

Under the moon,
Amour...I spell your name.

Under the velvet sky,
Amour... I breathe your soul.

Under the never-ending stars,
Amour...I dare your darkest gaze,
Into my breath.

How can I live
forever in your heart?

For nothingness
is surrounding my emptiness,
Firmness on my lips,
Deserted beyond your vast imaginations.
I stay in my anxiety.

For my greedy hands,
are now asking for your forgiveness,
For my desires
are unquoted under your beloved feet,
For my soul is darkness,
under your sincere veil.

How I shall share my life barrenly,
without your serene soul?

I come to you like a lonesome moonlight,
into your unconsciousness,
till you find my shadowy love,
under your igniting kiss.

Rusty Chains

Charlene Phare

Those rusty chains have weathered
Stained with my sodium tears
Crimson powders endeavoured

Decaying links now severed
Amidst chaos and the fears
Old rusty chains have weathered

Anchored to floating feathers
Cognitively probing spheres
Crimson powders endeavoured

Increasing inner pressure
Survival throughout the years
Those rusty chains have weathered

Life upon earth is measured
Sorrowfulness disappears
Crimson powders endeavoured

Each moment truly treasured
Tension released and clears
Crimson powders endeavoured
Those rusty chains have weathered

The Seasons

George Valler

Stop the clock, turn back the hour
Summer now reclaims her power
Spring has raised her weary head
From Autumn's slumbered wintry bed
Nature now her chance to reign
Calls forth the blossomed rolling plain
Life so shouts, rain falls the shower
River flow the daylight hour
Forest blaze, the leaf hidden calls
The majesty of tree lined halls
From blue the sky, soft clouds will roam
The glimmering sea, the rolling foam
A Heaven's need, in Nature's race
Soon winter calls to claim in haste

Mademoiselle

Nan DeNoyer

Mademoiselle could not forget the evening spent.
It was simply a most fantastic event.
We danced under a canopy of a million stars.
'Moonlight becomes you' he said.
He had sent an engraved invitation it read.
The house of Dupree invites you to the ball.
It was held in a most luxurious hall.
He pinned white roses on her tiny wrist
As they listened to the music of Franz Liszt.
He guided her across the ballroom floor.
She could not help herself she wanted more.
She wondered was this a romantic tryst?
This maiden fair it would be her first kiss.
Whimsical thoughts circled around her head.
From fantasy books she had just read.
Magical the evening more than she dreamed.
Looking at her roses she continued her dream.

46

Upper Westside

Steve Heins

1

I knock around Upper Westside
visit imposing Columbia campus,
yesterday.

I couldn't resist
returning to the place
where I grew up...
intellectually.

Today, NYC is 92 and humid.

2

It's time for Jack Kerouac
and Allen Ginsberg's
watering hole.

The West End Bar
a draft of beer:
Walls are slather
with photos of them.

3

I commune with the Beats
on the road
in my head,
howling.

New Day
Brandon Adam Haven

On bended knees with my head lowly bowed
Pleading to *The Lord* as I cried aloud
For mercy, peace, health and love
All the things my life has been so void without
But no longer had I finished this mournful prayer
I looked up before me and gazed into a specter's glare
I touched its hand and it carried me away
Contorting the dimensions through a hazy clay
We surged into infinity, there I begged to stay
With tears in my eyes I awoke to a brand new day

Skeletons
Susan Ila Davis

You seemed to be a walking wound
Dripping sadness from your fingertips
You always crave an eclipse
For it will shadow all the pain.

Scavenged memories left in boxes
Placed them there so you felt hollow
Up dark stairs we would not follow
Yet these skeletons will live again.

All were left with many questions
Are the answers in dark corners?
Did you perchance see the mourners
Crying tears meant for the real you?

On one orange September morning
When our lips drank of our first kiss
This records our apocalypse
When first our lovers souls were spied.

Said you were one dimensional
We both knew that to be a lie

Here is the truth now when you died
Because skeletons will live again.

Told me my words could make you cry.
Why'd your life become so remiss?
We could love you, but you dismiss
Beautiful love that was lent to you.

Amongst the dusty motes of light
That crept in as your life ebbed
Glance your form in window cobwebbed
It's a fanciful thought from me.

No wish for you to be stagnant
Pray your soul to be nomadic
Not lingering in this attic
Take our prayers and travel light.

Seasons Change

Girija Menon

Seasons change
Trees shed leaves, turning the page
Browns will soon sport tiny greens
Greens in shades many ....show off their sheens
Buds will flower in colors vibrant
Filling the tree, creating energy buoyant
The sky, a witness to all of this
Clouds in shapes unique glide in bliss
At times you see a smile up there
Pause, look up, and for a few seconds just stare
You will probably see faces or hear whispers
That's the beauty of silent beepers
Nature is quiet, yet force filled
Mess not with this energy ....remember
— you are not even billed
You care for it, it returns in multiples
It's all you have, enjoy the beauty
of the flight of bubbles

sediment of sentiments
Matt Elmore

sediment of sentiments roll on
stones long buried deep now push up
down from sources unseen spring
around bends not intended but there
drawn seeping through cracks in solid walls
saturate this stubborn cemented ground
grown hard from dry troubles of days
mocked by jaded rejuvenations immobilized
stuck in messy muds of moments uncovered
liberate now libations lost to lack of rain
rain rain rain drops ripple about rocks
stream on minerals essential to grow
as lank lessons slip slowly into the sea
run sweet memories of courses lost to time
as your beds change so do your shores
to wallow in winsome waters never ending
intended to shape more than just the land
but to intensify the flow of forever mercies so…
sediment of sentiments roll on

Stunned
Steve Heins

Sometimes, ignorance is
too loud,
too vacuous,
too lawless.

I am stunned into silence.

Yet
Gregory Richard Barden

oh why do you yet haunt me so?
your ghosts will never let me go
deep in the night from far below
they turned my dearest dreaming
as sprites of moonlight, scheming

oh why do you still come to me
and make me ache to break and be
more hopes lost to that endless sea
and drowned for sake of needing
your dark to leave me bleeding?

just when it feels you've left my heart
your spirit rends it wide-apart —
an open wound, served a la carte
when daylight comes to waken
lost 'midst the morrows, taken

you wander, wild, this 'bysmal brain
beneath these lands of counterpane
to bring me morns so daubed with rain
four-tens of years from leaving
this somber soul's still grieving

oh would I could, I'd kill them, cold —
love's fancy flights a dream can mold
though if the truth be plainly told
they're dearer me than morning
those phantoms midst their borning ...

those phantoms, You.

Cold Night
Fouzia Sheikh

This night is cold;
Heavy rain showers,
Flashes of lightnings,
Howling winds!

The heart is silent;
Sadness within,
Hurts and pains,
Broke it open!

Silence and emptiness;
Bring this night
Sleeplessness,
Eyes a bright!

Everything seems
To be foggy white
The dark horizon's
Fading out of sight.

Cold sleepless night;
Has tempted this
Broken heart,
With swift flights!

The Veil

Marie Harris

Beneath the veil of her pain
Tomorrow looms in a dying destiny
Fate allowed no mercy shown
Where the mantle of grief hangs heavily

Etched upon her face an agony born
Time suspended in a frozen frame
Floating in a sea of melancholy
An entity without a name

Flashes of the used to be, linger
When happiness was a sweet bliss
His face imprinted forever on her mind
The remembered flavor of his daily kiss

Clothed in unforgettable memories
Of a life lived in love sublime
The sweet melody of life was played
One sweet note at a time

Swirls of darkness threatening
An ice cold rain on the horizon
Hungry for sips of her pain
Death was secure in its mission

Taking the breath from her soul
Tethering her to the question why
Sleepwalking into tomorrow
With a heart that can't say goodbye

Decadence
Terry Bridges

Quizzical, each answer ticked off the question box
An evening hobby dedicated to the wildest furies
At present, quiescent, before the moon rocks

Pandora's children spilling in the Spring breeze
Dead, mortified creatures break the safe-locks
Testing the boundaries of patience and peace

Once beyond, an event-horizon crossed
Demons, ghouls, malignant escapees
Overrun like lemmings suicidally lost

Stirring up your mind's darkest memories
A death foretold as the temperature frosts
Blinded, devastated, brought to your knees

Each living thought verdigrised and mossed
The fetid atmosphere smelling of anti-freeze

Frozen in Time
Matt Cording

Frozen in time cradled in space
Diffused light illuminates your face
Your love for me a perfect display
Holding you close throughout the day
Please never leave me to be alone
We live together in our one bed home
Ok I get it you write the rules
But I can play nice I can be cool
I love the wonderful gifts you leave
But the headless ones are hard to believe

All with a Quiet Stillness
Steve Wheeler

Reflecting gold against bucolic wood
A fuse of light evokes a dappled charm
Defies the slated grey of agéd princes
Falling low as only inky shadows could
In shyness mellow harmony convinces
Shields a reckless heart from idle harm

Thin tissues of this solitude remain
All with a quiet stillness must it brood
To fold itself into a deep wood twilight
Imprisoned by illusion's tender chain
Suspended or deceased in stranger rite
The colours of the jaded hours allude

A savage orchestration of such love
In the subtle flavours of a beckoning
Meek petrichor arising from its surface
So floats its faint adornment like a dove
With scent so reminiscent of burnt lace
Ascending up toward its final reckoning

Drop All The Clocks
Tom Cleary

Drop all the clocks in clashing chime.
I'm through romanticizing time.
Since it only conceives death
I will not waste another breath.

Instead I'll live in the present flow
where precious seconds in me glow
in prismed point of pristine prime
ethereal in timeless clime.

Scapegoat Aptitudes

Aaron Blackie

He relished the stardom status,
Built on the hunchbacks of the naked
And the vulnerable ...

An apostle of the scapegoat syndrome,
The core leverage grounds, crested for
His crafty survival instincts ...

Master manipulator, who rides
On the back of cheap currencies, carved
Out of our short-sighted spectacles ...

Of the narrowed telescope that beckons
Us to view a magnified eclipse
Of the sun into a fully rounded sun ...

When out of that confined glimpse, we
Doggedly grind out the clued choices,
Leading to our feet hanging in limbo ...

The master craftsman riding on
The wind of the scapegoat syndrome,
Smartly takes our eyes of the course ...

To the gathered clouds nearby,
Blaming it for the deceptive eclipsed,
Calling for the destructive east wind ...

To the obliteration ... but be not beguiled,
All are caved in for the long and painful
Rides: Like the beginning that began the

Beginnings of the blame games;
One on subtle ground, approached the
Curiously willing another and the other ...

In vulnerable connectivity,

Was grafted into the tree of inclusivity ...
Threesome varied judgements awaited

The threesome stage players —
Serpent Eve and Adam —
outside the gate
Of their peaceable habitation ...

By the Watchman that sees,
Beyond the bulwarks and barricades
Of trickery!

Overflow

Imelda Zapata Garcia

when greatness sits in disarray
when genius lies untouched, at bay
while these neglected people pray
to touch the base of those who play

a varied number, slips through the crack
of some who might have found the knack
to function in a world with lack
of recognizing the greater stack

a cup of wonder filled to brim
to be sipped right up to the rim
to be swallowed by a righteous whim
by those who spy the awe in them

a spectrum note of different cord
which hold much more than common hoard
it spills the brilliance to afford
this world with promise to move toward

Writer's Ego

Susan Ila Davis

Excuse me for the state I'm in.
I've never been in such a place
I'm caught in unfamiliar skin.
Try to handle this with some grace.

I'm not sure what was expected
You have a strange reality
Now you seem to have rejected.
We lack compatibility…

I'm smart, I know who I should trust
I don't need to get your reference.
I am not here to fight or fuss.
We clearly have different preference.

Is a control thing that you do
To talk over others words.
Only do what is good for you
It becomes just a bit absurd.

From what I hear it's excepted
we're to be kind and never cruel
But your words are not accepted
You played me, I am not a fool.

Is it confidence, versus know-it-all?
Let me think on that a minute.
I'm old enough to make this call.
It's the latter, we won't spin it.

Words can be used to vent and feel.
It all depends on how they are penned
Some leave little to be concealed
Some are used to mend and commend.

Forgive me for the state I'm in.
On their ego do we slather

In accolades, when verse is thin
When sometimes is just blather?

Guess I am trying to explain
but not sure you will comprehend.
You tried to reign me and contain.
I was just a rainy day friend.

Remembrance
Archie Papa

Marking time with memories
immersed in the splendor of light
joy has the palette of color unbound
while sorrow has black and white

Moments fill the days gone by
as the years all line in a row
Silhouettes motion in jagged gaps
while color moves soft and slow

Love is the richness in memory
that fills in the shadows of pain
If fear should bring the darkening sky
then hope should bring the rain

Frame by frame the image starts
the essence of time completes
A mind will count the days and years
a spirit will count the heartbeats

Generations

Eric Aguilar

By the word of a poet,
and Alcazar of the alphabet,
and from the spirit to the abomasum,
come phrases, blissful of no fret.

It's your heart in recollect
of all the memories to find,
in which the poet's verse is elect,
in rhythm, rhyme, and time.

The heart speaks
and sings with the soul.
Life exists in the many
epochs of seeds sewn.

Switching Sides

Patti Woosley

When everything you do
is something you dread,
just blame it on waking up
on the wrong side of the bed.

Tomorrow you won't have
to neither cry nor hide
if you simply wake up
on the other side.

sailing on strange
Matt Elmore

stalking stages with pages of gazes
hemming up missing persuasions of time
whiskers account for wages of phases
lessons smack hard like traces on a behind
change is welcome — some is not so kind

words played like notes tend to entertain
yet feelings in between quotes remain
vulnerabilities in boats sailing on strange
strengths obliviously float over waves of gain
as humanity continues to promote this game

poetry like medicine may heal when applied
hustling fond memories to steal when supplied
stubborn cracks in wheels held up with pride
pure truth often reveals what we seek to hide
as layers begin to peel to the real core inside

songs exist sung to the delight of a few fans
despite what they've become to artists' exams
performed undone to financial demands
wounds cut deep on some despite the jams
when hunters stand hunted in worldly hands

Every Grace Filled Breath
Suzanne Newman

With every breath that He's exhaling,
I feel death's fear is less impaling,
And every breath that *He* breathes in,
Eases the weight, of *my* own sin.
With every pained and struggled gasp,
I'm loosened more from Satan's grasp,
And with each Messianic sigh,

I'm gifted hope from God most high.

With every mortal, suffering groan,
My soul's connected to His moans,
I see that Jesus, on the cross,
Relieves *my* debt and pays *all* cost.
With every Holy breath *He* breathes,
My faith does swell, as I believe,
At every tortured, little whimper,
My love and awe of Him grows deeper.

For with each Holy puff of air,
My burdens ease, as does despair,
And every movement from *His* lungs,
Ensures transgressions are far-flung.
I get a sense of pain and loss,
As I watch Jesus on the cross,
I feel bad that as I breathe in,
I'm saved, by passing *Him* my sin.

With every conquering gasp of air,
I feel His grace and divine care,
And every mumbled, human sigh,
Makes my heart leap and want to cry.
I thank you, Christ, for saving me
With every lamb's breath that you bleed,
For as you hang in victory, dying,
My soul shares in *Your* glory...flying.

So, thank The Lord, for Holy breaths,
That rescue us from sin's dark death,
'It is finished!' is His winning yell,
Which redeems souls from gates of Hell.
And, so, now I will use my jaws,
To sing all praises to The Lord,
So grateful that His earthly sighs,
Shout faithful promises, divine.

The Poetic Indigo
Tony Dukeva

Created in absolute solitude
By the eloquent poet, who's never quite clear
Conveyed in multi-layered aptitude
A concept that can be thoroughly weird
A concept about idyll and fantasy

Supreme to the point that dazzles the mind
Authentic about ethic integrity
A concept that drifts into the sublime
That inkling transposes every bit in your brain
Your soul changes colours
Your thoughts change their ways.
Empirical findings are not root of it

Theoretical postulations are the things you commit
You need more abstraction, more time to submit
For it is a notion of mental tooltip
Weaving together sanity and insanity
And more of insanity than soundness and wit
Oftentimes misunderstood by humanity
Belittled and thrown in an underground pit

And people can never be totally certain
If this is a madness or this is a gift
The mad hatter or the genius person,
Which definition perfectly fits
For the one who is destined to see
With indigo all the sensations
And hastily paste them with ink
on a white paper location.

Discontented Sonnet
Iain Strachan

I cannot conjure up a sonnet now
So little time to make a worthwhile theme
I look upon myself and see my brow
Is furrowed in the bid to dream a dream.

Ten lines to go and inspiration's dry
Each syllable's a strain to squeeze it out
At five more mediocre feet, I sigh
'I don't know what this poem's all about!'

So maybe nothing's what I'll end up saying
A zero-content poem might be great
Pad it out with platitudes and praying
Readers find a reason not to hate.

So ends this strange attempt, devoid of thought
That ends up meaning nothing, zero, nought.

Death Sleeps
Rafik Romdhani

Death sleeps under the eyelids
and wakes up early before the sun.
What must be done is a list of works,
without the knowledge of anyone.
Death may lurk in our breath
to dance dances along the path
and forever kisses whom it embraces
without meaning to do them harm.
It is what really draws the curtain
and makes mouths fall into silence.
Death sleeps under the eyelids
and wakes up early before the sun.
It must be the gentlest riddance
that closes dreams at the break of dawn.

—

My Heart Only is Able to See
Rafik Romdhani

I can hardly open my eyes
tired of devouring things
that my heart only is able to see.
But a dawn-like apple suddenly falls
into the sea and fascinates me.
I madly run towards fate's fruit
with my mouth glued shut effortlessly.
My eyes only look into the dream
candles blooming inside like poppies.
The sun outside is an eternal lie,
a mere crater for the hell we roam around.
My heart: my only ember, my battleground
against the lame invasions of the unknown.
I see everything right from here,
everything, no matter how unclear.

Seasons of Life
Lucille A. LaRoche

In transient
moments in time
l feel her near
a long awaited return
the vision of
her porcelain face
her eyes lowered
adorned to perfection
with her arched black
silken brows highlighting
her lowered eyelids of
soft velveteen eyelashes

always those long strands
of hair flowing like ribbons
that once caressed my face
as her coral pink lips softly
softly met mine that
time can't efface

a beautiful beach rose
petal flew away one day
swiftly like a petal within
a summer breeze to a
distant shore unexpectedly

the season of lives
altered that day

time doesn't stop
your heart doesn't
the world still spins
on its axis
as you stand still

till the tides of the sea
in synchrony with the
with the phases of the moon
and the powers that be
capture me within a
summer breeze
to a distant shore
we will meet in
our eternal season

It is Finished

Steve Wheeler

'It is finished' sounds so final
like a nail knocked into wood
and on most days it would seem
like all your work came to no good
but in one dramatic instance
on a dark Judean hill
those three words signalled triumph
as a watching world fell still.

'It is finished' whispered almost
into silence like defeat
but the utterance was a victory
where the light and darkness meet.
'It is finished' was a statement
of a work brought to completion
of redemption and salvation
and the act of sin's deletion.

For crying out loud
there's no funeral shroud
and no grief is allowed
by the loud screaming crowd
and his head has been bowed
by a cruel thorny crown
and his back has been ploughed
'neath his dark purple gown
but he won't make a sound
and his heart isn't cowed
and he will not back down
no he will not back down.

It is all finished now
it is over and done
and the battle's been won
by the conquering son
and what he has begun
two millennia has run

it is finished it is done
by the hands
by the hands
by the hands of the Risen One.

Soft, the Bells

Gregory Richard Barden

soft, soft, I ring the bells
soft, the bluebells blooming
softer tho', her pleading eyes
with each breath, consuming ...

hark, hark, I call to thee
hark, so blushes morning
hearken to her linen cheek
crimson as the borning ...

haste, haste, alas the years
haste to cut the bracken
hasten, to her dimming gaze
'for the shadows slacken ...

hush, hush, I whisper yet
hush to bide the nether
hushing now, her angel voice
gone, my love ... forever.

I Died with You that Day

Kirsty Howarth

You're now gone
And I'm left with all this pain
My days are so lonely
And I think I'm going insane

You're no longer here
But every day I try
To move on with my life
But all I do is cry

The one thing I have
Are the photos that remain
Hanging on my wall
But they just bring more pain

I got down on my knees
And I prayed that you could stay
But my prayers were unanswered
And instead, I died with you that day

Every moment without you
Gets harder but I try
I've been trapped in this nightmare
Since the day I said goodbye

When I sleep at night
I see you in my dreams
But your image fades as I awake
And nothings as it seems

I now walk alone
Strolling about town
I still search for you
And my worlds turned upside down

I got down on my knees
And I prayed that you would stay

But my prayers were unanswered
And I died with you that day

I have to accept
That I need to set you free
And I have to accept
That you can no longer be with me

Broken promises
As our story had to end
Tears and regrets
And a heart that's still to mend

I got down on my knees
And I prayed that you would stay
But my prayers were unanswered
And I died with you that day

The Trail
Angel Thomas

I walk
In this long way
Across oceans, over hills
Following the path of my dream
My heart is certain of where I'm going

Storms strike
Acidic rain dissolves the hope
But my avidity gathers it again

I walk on...
Forward ever, backward never
The gold of future beckons me
It is past giving up

Eclectic Ballroom
Graeme Stokes

Reflective locks, the moss clad cannels,
aperture for tomorrow's dreamers
Weeping willows imbibe the whimsical vibe,
of deep thinkers and light sleepers

Cobblestones leading all points trendy,
meander of a throng of mellow
Funkadelic haze the fabric of the chilled,
choreographed peccadillos

Horses for courses the non-conformists,
lunch with no fixed abode
Tattoos rebel yell, taboos can go to hell,
radicals break the mould

Old guard to avant-garde,
a box of quirky charms
Take you back tracks you sorta recollect,
duel for your open arms

The realm of the nonchalant the fancy free,
the purists love to hate
Those stuffy platitudes dressed in blue,
can stay at home and wait

The state of independence, the 'so what' buzz,
running on Valium time
Skulls and bones sticks and stones,
short plank for the diatribe

I hear you buck and stables,
a most unconventional voice
North London bound for kindred sound,
a top alternative choice

———

Only but a Dream...

Praise Edwin

I had a dream,
broken mirrors thrown into streams
of mild consciousness and thought;
In the darkness of light they often gleam,
revealing themselves as slaves already bought!

I had a dream,
we were divided yet functioned as a team
till a point that we could not;
we could barely pipe down our boiling steam
that boiled and cooked meat in the heart of our pot!

I had a dream,
my darkness was covered by a radiant beam,
I had figured that it was bound to be my lot;
In my sorrows she was my cream,
her beauty glowing and her brain so hot!

I had a dream,
In your absence my ink flowed into reams,
In my cold loneliness you were my only cot;
my life of late has been a seam
because you were the only one I've got!

I had a dream,
You were sitting next to me
the stars above us seemed like dots;
Midnight, on a boat far into the black sea —
your beautiful face shimmered like a that of a tot!

I had a dream,
We drank whiskies or so it seems
though it wasn't enough but your face was to my pain a jot;
We made a toast and sang some hymns
in the wedding party of Sir Hugglesbot!

Cheers to the days you were here,

cheers to the times we were a sweet pair;
I had a dream about you last night;
how we danced sensually under the white moonlight—
Those times will forever be in my heart!

Whirling Dervish
Karin J. Hobson

Spinning earth? Dervish birth,
Journey to Divinity;
Round and round, arms out
Taken to unknowns.

Planets spin so does man
Yet, does not understand,
Mysteries behind each twirl
Unlock secret worlds.

Accompanied ecstasy
Succumbing to adventure;
Dervish man loses time and spin,
To enter other realms.

Mystics talk of higher grounds,
Where compared to here,
Is like singing songbird,
With no song to sing.

Ever is Dervish dance
Reaching worlds unknown;
Only to return,
With valued lessons learned. Blessings!

Trails of Hope

Sarah Wheatley Tillbrook

The effervescent healing trail
Of the butterfly.

Lands so tenderly
Upon a branch syncopated from its core
Mother
yet breathing in harmony with the breath
Of the Earth

It clings loosely
To its spot
Tended to by the
Soft arms of the wind
Gently playing on its antennae

Wings flap strong against the motion of the breeze

We stop
The butterfly pauses but for an instant.

Waiting for its fellows
To join in its path
Towards some light.

Some light we watch and wait
And subsume and multiply
into warmth and hope

We stop
We wait

And we are still

In the effervescent healing trail of the butterfly

Till Life Do Us Part

Kene Orenye

Hungry, broken throttles this lurid loop
Devoid of truth of happiness of hope
Stories unfinished lives unfulfilled
Miserable memories in hearts stencilled
And mind blank seeking a purpose to live for
So methought or so with truth me fought

I wrote a song only phantoms will dance
Maybe men too if reason might glance
Intimacy on earth me sought to naught
Was I the lowliest of men, had I not a heart?
Sing a song of an ol' boy who's gone
Found a lover, Lola, a sweet soul once born

Maybe I found joy or whatever feeling this is
For once mine to keep, her presence a bliss
Like heavy scents of rum on a gay mind
A sign of pure love that is called mine
Till life do us apart is my song for Lola
We sang we loved we danced the hula

Melodic Memories

Charlene Phare

Music chiming from yesteryear
Tuneful melodic memories
Recalling past times, falling tears
Music chiming from yesteryear
Melancholic notes, relayed fears
Playing throughout the centuries
Music chiming from yesteryear
Tuneful melodic memories

It Hurts

Angel Thomas

It hurts that you are leaving me this way
It hurts that you leave in the darkest day

It hurts that you promised a lot
Yet now leaving when the handle is hot

It hurts that you leave me in the scaring dark
It hurts as I can't find my way back

It hurts that our dreams lie scattered
The future is blurry, my heart is shattered

It hurts that you leave me for another
It hurts, for you made me a mother

It really hurts, oh it hurts so deep
It cuts keenly — I cannot sleep!

Today

Christopher Mercon

I would slip into the sky
Just to feel the rain's cadence
upon the ethereal skin of my soul —
to feel the billowing
of my gossamer sail
upon the whispering wind,
and to bask in the warm sun
of this glorious, windy morning.

Warrior Square

Graeme Stokes

Ground rules set in outlined chalk
Of broke crackpipes and tomahawks
Ghost dancing eyes jut out on stalks
They follow everywhere you walk
There's glares from the stairs, well I declare!
Better watcha step down at warrior square!

Insults shoot at obtuse angles
From dry mouths on jingle jangles
Bus shelter stoops down bent and mangled
Playing it straight just proved new-fangled
The needy shake for an urgent repair
Some devil may care, down at warrior square!

Bombed out trees are throwing shapes
And don't want to elucidate
Why the wasted past just can't escape
From flying pigs and early graves
You can catch my drift, it's in the air!
Who said life is fair, down at warrior square!

Wings cling on prayers to a vexed Madonna
Just weapons of choice no code of honour
The law is sussed by skittish coppers
That the sane are walking cannon fodder
Your luck has just been caught in their snare!
On their cross to bear, down at warrior square!

Signs designed for bloods and crips
On bitter shoulders with angry chips
Hip flasks drown the sinking ships
Long since capsized from a fragile grip
An SOS cries out in despair!
From a smoking flare, down at warrior square!

River
Tom Cleary

Body of water
wimple of wave
dimple in the
aqueous eye of time
borne of oval ocean
seminal sea
generated in jungles
fermented fens
fine flagellations
worlds within wombs
amniotic ampules expanding
trickles of toes
headwaters pooling
until saturated
it tumbles toward
forwarding falls
glimmering shimmer
gurgling gulps of glee.

Thinking
Terry Bridges

In the cool rhythm of my contemplation
Words occur like deep-sea creatures from the depths
Fabulous to behold and comprehend in earnest
Awaiting their birth among the myriad fishes
Exhilarating excitement in each tortured breath
Each in its place, flotsam and jetsam, life and death

A Song of Light and Dark

Dale Parsons

Heed the words of this dark song,
A forwarding made to all.
For all who remain in a place too long,
Consider the ancient Wall.
Once was sturdy, once was strong,
Now crumbles, fit to fall.

The builder who, now long gone,
Proud of his endeavour.
A marvel raised where it belonged,
Built to last forever.
Lost now to an age bygone,
The curse of time and weather.

Heed the words of this dark song,
Heed a warning call.
Wither the ones, who won't move on,
Corrosion eats them all.
For those who remain in a place too long,
Will crumble like old walls.

Rejoice the words, a song of light,
A spark can set you free.
For those who leave the dull for bright,
Consider the birds in trees.
From their perch, from great height,
Imagine what they see.

Many the bird, delight in flight,
Proud, their wings of feather.
A marvel soars, by day by night,
Looks down on fields of heather.
Free are their minds, free is their sight.
When free, the bonds that tether.

Rejoice the words, a song of light,
These words to help you see.

———

That as the birds, enjoying flight,
So could you and me.
For those who leave the dull for bright,
Forever will be free.

A Sheath
Karin J. Hobson

Most shall wear black or white
Of, Bride or Mourner's cape
Many will make actions right
Others profiting in mistakes.

But, where does thy soul lay
When numbered days arrive
And, you take a breath of Truth
And, are ruthlessly denied?

Do you rebound on your own
With a bewailing groan
Or, perhaps a simple lapse
In a judgemental synapse?

Oh, of cloak and dagger
Lest ye bent on tyrannic anger
Take thee hold in other hand
A sheath with solid stand.

For, brave is he with steed
And, will with driven feed
To mount a hailstorm of,
And, still come out above.

The Depth of Loss
Marie Harris

The depth of loss
A deep dark abyss
Abstract colors
Dressed in black
A vast desert of airless skies
A weight of smothering emotions
Knife slicing pain, torturing the mind
Nerve endings tangled and twisted
Emptiness is an endless dark
Whips of fire flay the soul
Seeking anonymity deep within
Refuge from the blinding truth
Drifting in an endless chasm of unrelenting pain
Grief slips quietly into your bones
Like a whisper of wind across an ancient tomb
Stripping you down to naked fear
Feeling every little nuance of pain
Breath suspended in a silent scream
Fading into numb
Colors bleed to grey
Eyes dry as sand
Gritty tears etch a path
Upon grief ravaged cheeks
Grief slowly devouring
Consumed by a deluge of memories
Darkness plagues the shattered mind
Somewhere beyond comprehension
Today is lights out, solitary quiet is sought
Someday, tomorrow will grant a lessening
of grief on that distant horizon

Absence Makes the Heart Grow Fonder

Geoff Stockton

It's hauntingly weird,
but just as fascinating …
the way you just seem to show up
in my classroom dreams …
sometimes too, latter-day adult nightmares
you continue to show up in those 'Sliding Doors'
junctions in my life…

You find the 'gaps' the vulnerable spaces
my intangible need for your company…
short, brief spurts in secretive places…
a 'Hello' or 'Hi' here and there
an occasional 'I miss you'…
keeping me pulled into your gravity
then, once again…
Returning to hiding yourself in privacy.
Your illusive presence has survived through
too many years.

When will be
our final get-together?
Yet another 'overdue' catch-up,
and why?
Should we not change this lifetime of 'catch-ups'
Recognising our real shared need of
loving life together.

Adrift at Sea

Lucille A. LaRoche

By the sea
I sail away deep
within my inner self
to the whispers
of their gentle swells
lapping a rhythmic
melody against the shore
soothing my soul
like a lullaby
with my friend the sea

I just drift away in solitude
with the salty sea spray
permeating my inner being
navigating to a distant shore
in unison with the currents
and swells of the sea
encompassed within a quiescent
womb in a soothing timeless
space

Adrift
at sea
my soul
and I
where
peace
resides

The Sum of it All
Michael Balner

As rays of light form a star
As raindrops become a sea
So will each single self in my
mind become the whole of me

As a night swallows the shadows
As a vacuum swallows the sounds
So will the voracious black hole in
me swallow my black rotten heart

As a sum of wounds becomes death
As small acts of good become love
So will the sum of all bad and good
Become the ultimate life

Filament of Light
Eric Aguilar

It is not
the filament of light
that opens the flower...
you see, before the sun even rises,
songbirds sing of their love to the bloom
and, in turn, the stamen opens to
reveal the blossom's filament.
The trust of these buds are
in the fiber of their being.

Day's Eye

Sarah Wheatley Tillbrook

I pick a daisy
Torn between
The days that are
And days that were

My thoughts stand hazy
Mind unclear
My present scarred
By thoughts of her

I was once amazed
By days eye seen
Now all joy is far
And hand grips firm

For my sweet Daisy
Once turned to me
Broke love forevers
My thoughts unlearned

By sweetness played me
As daisy's white leaf
Found another lover
Set for new earth

I stand here lonely
Waiting for peace
Hoping for clovers
To rebuild my worth.

Dusty Walk
Geoff Stockton

Time lazily idles by
in the Tuscan hills, a landscape
untroubled by modernism,
stress, pace and bustle.
The earthy red heat
reflects back from ancient
roofs and the walls of villages
roosting on hill-tops.

Vineyards fall away
from rolling hillsides...
you can almost smell
the musky Chianti presses
at work in the farms below.
Our old dusty and stony
track meanders on it seems forever,
through this vine-clad landscape.

We pass ripening olives
swelling in the heat
neatly arranged lizard groves,
while fields filled with sunflowers
track the rays of the setting sun
to the smouldering west
beyond Florence.
Eventually the unique outline of
St Gemignani comes into view
with its eccentric imposing towers...
historical winding streets with stuffed
hogsheads and other
local gastronomic delicacies
hanging forlornly.
The strung-out

village shops dwindled and gave way to
timeless monastery cloisters,
captivating those of us lucky enough
to discover his deftness of
Andrea Pizza's dextrous fingers and the
haunting cadences of his
ethereal harp music.

Unsurprisingly, the
fragile plucked notes
and haunting melodies
still linger in my soul
long after the dusty track
walk that embodied all that was
the spirit, art and music of
Chianti Classico Italy.

Circus Parade
David Knauss

Cotton candy clouds float by
Zephyr wind propels them across an azure sky
My imagination sees a circus parade
A calliope leads this promenade
Lions, tigers, and bears in gilded wagons proceed
With performers mounted on prancing steeds
Giant elephants moving as trunks trumpet loud
Announcing their arrival regally proud
Monkeys, gorillas, and even giraffes
My wild imaginings make me laugh
I imagine far off the calliope's tune
As the sun slowly gives way to the moon
My cloud borne parade soon has blown past
To me, the clouds disappear too fast
But before long my spirits lift
As I say thanks to God for this imagination gif

Anchor in Life's Storm
David Knauss

As the seas begin to broil and foam
Waves reach heights heretofore unknown
A Gale of enormous strength and width
Whirling overhead like a Dervish twist

The storm forecast must have missed the mark
This boat trip will be no lark
The Master has the sailors reef the sails
But even that's of very little avail

So the Master prepares a sea anchor
Not daring to risk the ship even more
The deck hands deploy it off the stern
Soon the ship made a gentle turn

Into the waves now riding each huge swell
What's the outcome is hard to tell
Will the sea allow them a safe trip
Or drag them under with Neptune's grip

Much like the Master is our Lord and Savior
Our Anchor throughout life's raging weather
In life's storm He anchors the world
No matter the weather He calms life's storm

Truth
Angel Thomas

A lie which with confidence is told
Gives the hearer assurance to hold
Where in truth's cloth, the lie
Smothers doubts, and they die
Till pen of time writes reality bold

Winds of Change

Joseph Andrew Miller

They built a ship to sail the world.
The allure is fair, the unending sea.

Though a bottled ship might never wear,
a traveller can't always be.

The ship is tall, and bounded true,
to match the deep, vast, warping waves.

The wind is harsh, pulling every thread
of sails as worn as galley slaves.

No journey is ever complete,
another destiny to be found.

Yet every ship, from any fleet
fears time as it counts down.

For a sailor may love the water,
yet the water would swallow him up.

While the ship collects its memories,
every splinter, tear, and crack corrupt.

So they take this ship of Theseus,
this weathered and salted beast,
and pry up every plank and rail,
replacing every single sail,
till nothing of her still remains.

Is she now deceased?

No.
I was that ship of oaken boards,
and tomorrow that ship will still be me.

Time Zones
Geoff Edwards

We're on different time zones
You are up when I am down
Connections between us solely
—are apps upon our phones

We're on different time zones
Sitting on dissimilar thrones
Each drummer beat—a cacophony of sound
We're on different time zones
You are up when I am down.

Silver Claw
Tony Dukeva

Impatiently my eyes turned upwards
Expecting there the crescent's awe
And there it stood, the quarter-moon,
resplendent like a silver claw.
That sparkling rise made an impression
the stars were bowing in the fog
the earth contracted its precession
when covered in an argent cloak.
Mystic, miraculous occasion
Fomented stormy mental flow
Of this phenomenal equation
Possessing all that splendid glow.

Solemn Stillness
Tony Dukeva

When the solemn stillness holds my thoughts,
And the yawning peace attempts to charm me,
Blissful reveries beseech for spot
Dreams of silent days disarm me.

Then sweet quietness steps as my guest
And tranquility beholds my fingers,
Eyes comfort in noiseless quests,
Screams are gone, the calmness lingers.

There Comes a Time
Shawn McGiniss

There comes a time
When you can look back
See yourself
Your past

You see who
Who you were
Who you are
The You you knew would last

Memories seen through
Your looking glass
Broken mirror you
So many views of you

Fervid Feelings
Rafik Romdhani

If time but halts wheels
while I am still wild and free,
If to my pondering eye
clouds just bend a knee,
from fervid feelings,
I will crack open a sea
and build a ship from poetry.

Give Me
Deborah Griffin Howard

give me
a reason to be blind
to everything left behind
when you told me
you were the one for me
and then you gave me
a reason to be blind

Photos
Dave Strudwick

Past
We took shots
But why, to stop time
or to capture, a futility
A joy and memories to the now
Looking from the opposite side of the tracks
I see a new perspective
Of the ship once sailed
I cannot go back
beauty remains
From where I
stand today

The Concerto of the Fire

Dale Parsons

Spirits lifted higher at the concerto of the fire,
A guitar and a voice, flames join the choir.
A tune is a tonic, a dose symphonic,
The cracking of wood adds a different sonic.
The orange flames dance, hypnotic show,
Light up your friends in a shadow glow.
Voices with flame, together weave around,
Melodies of colour and sound.

One thing that you need is a song,
And to sing that song to someone.

Sat around a fire with music and friends,
A flame and a voice, in harmonies blend.
Sat around a fire with good folk,
Singing of a song or the telling of a joke.
Faces of your friends, orange-hued,
Adding to their stories some mood.
Voices with flame, together they surround,
Medleys of colour and sound.

One thing that you need is a joke,
To smile and laugh with good folk.

Sat around a fire, share a good time,
Friendships and flame, together they shine.
Black against orange, a dark silhouette,
Images not so easy to forget.
Remembered long after its end,
The music, the fire and the friends.
Bonds unbroken, forever bound,
Memories of colour and sound.

One thing that you need is a tale,
To reminisce and regale.

My Sunday Color
Marie Harris

My Sunday color is streaked with rain
The sky dulled by rain clouds
The rhythmic patter of the falling rain
Cocoons me in a peaceful languor

The window pane glistens with silver raindrops
The Sunday color is green upon a luscious lawn
The trees waving their green in the bustling breeze
The silence soothes my Sunday soul

My Sunday color is blooming bright with faith
A slow moving day, listening to my voice within
Be thankful for this Sunday color of rain
Soon a bouquet of many fragrant colors will bloom

My Sunday color is mellow and subdued
Giving thanks for my many blessings of rainbow
shining
Simple quiet, nothing disturbing my peaceful color
Everyday my world spills crayon colors all around

City Clothesline
Joseph Andrew Miller

In the watered reflection, The City hangs
Tightly pinned to the shoreline
By those square shoulders on the ground
The tips of those buildings ripple
A dangling threat to fall down into deep sky
Till the wind builds up to a fright
To gust all those lights and dwellers away

To My Soul
Kwaku Adjei-Fobi

Yes!
The hare leaps between burrows.
The lair is its castle.
The rain can do its worst.
It thought about it first.

What about the tears?
It wells, falls, tears
a moment with its momentum,
yet the sparrow's song turns it off,
the sun's rays dry it up,
and the morning breeze lifts it high
on a dais to the maze Life is,
I'll find my way home!

My lore lies lean,
getting ready to fatten in the season.
It's just catching her breath
after all these slaloms,
graceful, still elevated
by her own endeavours.

Yes, the umbras may take a toll,
exact some altitude,
but a tot of light seeps through,
widening
beyond the encircling gloom!

Going My Way

Gregory Richard Barden

thick mist …

breath of dusk …
bearing its own tales
the yellow bricks wind away
swallowed by the brume
fallow footprints, long since faded
but I cared not to trace them anyway …
vacant souls searching for the
most basic of virtues
leading another young pilgrim to
fates unknown … and un-noted
(the fog itself endows more guidance)
… they never returned.

crossroads …
proverbial *and* actual
my instructions were clear, as always
the counsel, lucid and lettered
yet life has never borne the conventional
courses for me …
naught a prevailing wind or
timid tack to weigh …
regrets?
real as rain …
but they bear conscience and wisdom —
grateful, am I, for each.

night …
is closing in like a promise
the forest, deep, yawns forsaken
the lad in me longs for a sweet dream —
a fanciful lullaby
and final blink of lashes, soft …
but ambition is a jealous mistress
and she wrings complacency and excuse
from the hems of my spirit —

legacy and contrition dance the
dark like fireflies
love's wages howl in the night
chilling my thoughts, my marrow ...
my blood.

the choice ...
was made for me, long ago ...
before these serpentine paths were
packed and paved, the placement
of my steps was ordered ...
that road untraveled — of red brick and border
was written at time's inception upon
the binding of my soul
and there shan't be another ...

going my way.

You
Sarah Wheatley Tillbrook

Count not the offers in the air
Style not to entertain eyes stare
Whimsy not for featured edit
Dress up bold, or shy or comfy

Look not at the glare of others
Feel the warmth of pleasant summers
Confident in your own skin
Short, or tall, fat or thin

Be the soul attracts no attention
Other than kind introspection
Knowing you don't have to hide
For you love who you are inside.

You...My Words

Hisham Hawwa

I'm painting in the plural:
painting in a painting in a painting
mapping this memorial mensural
materializing this immortal mural...
while dancing, chameleon I became
framed in former flame...
a bohemian to the empyrean
a ballgame with multiple tasking...manually laboring
arousing the devils that live in distorted angels ...
brushed...push...touch... am another stranger,
piano prayed in the paranormal portrait ...
in the gait across the sidereal strait
being or becoming...living or loving...
being late...becoming fate'...
I feel...as your ribs rub my crotch...
the explanation to the itch...
on the ridge of my frozen fridge...
as I watch...stitching my unstitched wretch...
velvet verbs and verse...smiling beyond words
pelvis voice and volcano...versatile, wild birds
are dentelle on my table
hell...knell...pell...spell
able or fable to my foible
table pens poetry
table yens coffee
table paints mural
on the wall...
rains pains on aura of the floral
musicking in streets of the rural
me, seen by me
in malls...stalls... ...walls
— agora...in amphora,
in all faces...places...spaces...

[][][][][]

art needs the noise of typewriter
the bell of meowing
the cell of cocooning
the smell of cooking
the light of lightning
the blight of bloomer
the sight of a flower
the fight of a warrior
the taste of thinking
the waste of waiting —
a form of whole into a sole soul
diastole and keyhole...or keynote
aureole of camisole... or boat+port
diatonic or harmonic...or just ironic
palette and brush and easel...
socket and butch and chisel...
damsel...tinsel...morsel...
violin demands a dark violet varnishing
and resonant strings and pleadings
beestings...blowing...fillings
flourish...fetish...relish...and vanishing
horn of plenty...wheat...dates...
affinity and maturity...
beat...heat...bet and swear..
repeat...reheat...heartbeat...retreat
at the gate of the consummate
big dipper and amusement ride
slide on the tide of my beautiful bride
the curves of a Star...nerve of more far
dancing at night floor...by the dormant door...

[][{[][][]

You ...are me...
we are painting the portal in peace
the penumbra of our way...
we are daringly delineating in feast
the umbra of our day
the portrait...says...
stay inside ...in the picture...
keep the paradise of pleasure…
the tincture of the tuneful torture
having you in my heart,
You and my art...
with scenes so many…
umpteen are women
I only need ...
you and clef and chord
the notes of my music...
and trillo pod…
and theaters...vehicle...cars...
alabaster…chronicle…scars
horizon...haven…heaven
traffic...blue pills…note of seven
off-color...risqué…kiss you

[][][][][]

arms make hugs... of dozens of drugs
plug the already unplugged.
floods of rubs of spuds
eternal words...fly like birds
of no finality...and I know
there are so many thousands of things...
I only need two...
YOU...
and my vocabulary...
YOU…
and my melancholy…
YOU…
and my memory…

Beloved Taken

Karin J. Hobson

When world comes to an end,
And, clouds there are no more;
Stars have fallen to contend
With the Sun and Moon's roar;
Let, it be known this day forth
Love does exist after final wave
to shore.

For, what is this of Twin Flames
But, she who burns as he soars
Days alone whilst claiming
Spirit Realm both are known
And, may transmit in a state
Of innate intuitions honed

Oh, it's true few will clearly see
All talents given to each of thee
But, be assured you have heard
These loving remarks of
"I love you" from distant bird
In Destiny's Magickal surge.

And, upon love's earthly death
And, you are left to wander,
It'll be Destiny's ultimate plan
To render return to sender;
Your beloved taken when
Eternity had had other plans.

Indelible

Fouzia Sheikh

There are traces that
are indelible in time
Its measure is
not quantifiable and its
value is inscrutable.
You cannot measure
the trajectory of
His steps throughout
His earthly season.
Day and night meet memories
Not to forget the one who joyfully
never ceased
to preach passionately
regardless of the seasons,
sowed with tears,
and harvested songs
in the nations.
No one will be able
to match the size and weight
Of his footsteps that
marked the path
of revealed truths.
Deep I leave the seeds
that are sheaves
united in the hand of eternity.
Now your song
is eternal in the four winds
and your indelible mark
on the everlasting
Kingdom of Lord.

Unfinished
Rafik Romdhani

Life leaves us unfinished
after it has our backs bent
with those dreams we dreamt.
So many tasks on shoulders
do remain unaccomplished.
The future inside our minds
fallen finally in cement cities
to be locked up and hushed.
Life breathes in Man its ironies
and challenging contradictions.
The maelstrom of miscalculations
make one feel bashful and abashed.
The wise man never with transience
counts nor into far-fetchedness runs.
The spirit would fly after its willingness
if the helpless body crashed and burnt.
Life leaves us unfinished
after it has our necks wrung
between the red hammer of time
and the thick anvil of mud.
Life Leaves us unfinished.

Cold Remembrance
Jan Kenneth Velle

Cold remembrance...
Of an ice memory...
strong out taken from a seeing love
One that took your heart away
And left us all alone...
Just to visit the lost in time

The Poet
Michael Hislop

Elusive
Who is it?
Effervescent
What is
Enigmatic?
When Where How?

The bard
Singing the mystic
Scribbling the Pen
Enwrapped sentences
Wow, a magic carpet
Flying through time
Yours, Mine, Theirs

Shooting out alphabet
Spelling dreams
Welcome All-Seeing Eye
Glare anew
Bless Me
Your incendiary gaze

What is a Poet?
Wordsmith
Or DJ
Or Fisher of Men
Mixing memes
Weaving images
Truth or Dare

Is he a sword
Or she a shield
Accusatory tone
Or defender?

To encourage
Or to disparage
Questioning
To esteem
Or to offend
I wonder
Whose pleasure?
Whose treasure?

Is this poetic state
A mask
Some wicked shroud
Or a state of being
Because the word
Must be adorned
To walk amongst men?

Or is the poetic
A weeping wound
Far deeper than flesh
Bloodlust for ideas
For truth must live?

Or are we, the poets
Scientists of grammar
Our brothers' keeper
Sowing the seeds
In future Hearts
For the forest
To grow again?

Seeds of Sadness
Larry Bracey

Go ahead and water them,
Slowly watch it grow,
Take pride in your garden,
Because people reap what they sow,

Everything that was harvested,
Things you refused to sell,
Were freely given to those,
Who deserved to know your hell,

Your fruits both plump and juicy,
With bitterness to the core,
You watch them all consumed,
Until there wasn't any more,

Knowing those who feasted,
Each doing so without haste,
Filling their bellies til swollen,
Leaving not a scrap of waste,

They quietly slither away,
Taking a piece of you,
Replanting Seeds of Sadness,
The way that serpents do.

Gone to the Dogs
Graeme Stokes

The escalator's out of whack,
packed up and gone to Halifax,
there's squatter's rights for Pepsi max,
your eyes adapt and get the knack,
but feet won't seem to take the slack,

for the chap with gout and the lass with tracks!

The centre's gone to rack and ruin,
flagships need a major sprucing,
the next man don't know what he's doing,
footwear needs a proper shoe in,
it's Costa's last stand!
And there's trouble brewing!

Local parks are in a state,
of disrepair put on the slate,
the Odeons are second rate,
you just wanna sleep and hibernate.
The football ground just plays away,
down the road of retrograde,
they don't want to negotiate,
to clear the crap that's on display!

The roads are blown and gone to pot,
more holes than a lousy plot,
the drains don't wanna help a jot,
just spray you with a parting shot.
The fines are dropping like it's hot,
for ganja smelling parking lots!

The promises have come to nought,
for watering holes and roundabouts,
the unwashed have to do without,
just ponder what it's all about,
while sucking on a drooping snout!

The folks are told to wind their neck in,
as blind eyes glaze a redirecting,
deaf ears forever testing, testing,
for the helpless souls their representing,
but really what were you expecting?
A coat of arms in an honest setting?

For Such a Time as This
Aaron Blackie

For such a time as this —
Many are on the
Fast-paced lanes,
Lanes led on the
Plane of no plain field...
The eyes that see
Beyond the nose,
Eased our roaring
Temperaments....

For such a time as this —
When volatile are the lips
Of obduracy,
That stirred for a bang full
Of empty serration winds,
The feet must be weary
To gathered before podiums
Crafted for chameleon
Whisperers....

For such a time as this —
Scapegoat is the
Penny paid sacrifice,
Burnt at the altar of fools;
Then the crowbar crowd
Must rolled away the clouds,
That the face of the
Masquerade be made naked...

For such a time as this —
When dusty droughts loom
For the dance of doom
In longitudinal famine;
Fruit must become seed
For the soil, seedling fruits

Of many generations —
The ploughing breathe
Of resilient farmsteads...

For such a time as this —
The vulnerability of the
Times, knee genuflected
In the home of the
Colour blindness,
The harbingers
Of the narrowed
Mindedness tomorrows!

For such a time as this —
Patient watchfulness
Should much more be
The surging currents,
Upsurge subtly,
The chameleon cleverness;
The inordinate arousal
Of the beast in us...
For such a time as this...

For such a time as this —
The cloudy shadows
Of uncertainty,
Shall not loom
Over the horizon forever...
The rainbow colour
Shall makeups the dusty eyes
Of our hope's encircled
Space capsuled sky...

For such a time as this...

Restless Mind (Tired Soul)

Archie Papa

Restless mind, tired soul
nothing left in fates control
holding back the pace of time
death the punishment, life the crime

Restless mind, tired soul
bridges burned collect no toll
shattered pieces on the ground
all that's lost need not be found

Awake the soul, refresh the mind
sorrow sees the world unkind
chaos lives for worries gain
fear remembers only pain

Awake the soul, refresh the mind
gone the past so far behind
once the truth is understood
love will serve the greater good

Woe

Terry Bridges

The dreary night frosts my pain with sorrow
I can neither move nor rest
Fattened by pills to a gelatinous mess
Somehow I have to accept my fate
But inside I rebel like Lucifer in fury
My legs and feet are swollen and nothing fits me
The cracked rib creases with agony
My back is an Iron Maiden of torture
Hopefully the vertebrae will knit and heal in time
For now I suffer and try to climb into bed

Agenda
Geoff Edwards

Oh ye of words, oh ye of verse,
Oh ye of agendas putting them first.
Your words, the words of silver and gold,
Heard again and again, in the palace, of the oversold.

The message, the mighty mountains echo in thunder,
Of the love you have put asunder.
The flash of the bolt, lighting up the sky,
Shelter I crave, shelter I long for, in the palace of why.

The gale from the north, cold northerlies spume,
Flame from the candle extinguished, it's dark as a tomb.
Cut from a sabre, smooth, silky, flashing, swift,
No anchor to hold, no foundation to stand, in the palace of adrift.

The bridge is aflame, ablaze, twisting and tangled,
No path will be trod, all routeway is strangled.
On the rocks of despair, on a bed of nails,
No hand to grasp, no shovel to dig, in the palace of travails.

For this is my fate, for this is my existence,
To forage one crumb, of merger subsistence.
Crawling creeping crunching upward, on broken glass,
Throwing open the doors, throwing upward the sash,
in the palace of impasse.

Jubilee
Steve Wheeler

I'm breathing,
though my febrile brain
is searching through the futile mess
for meaning from insanity.
This potentate
has stumbled in his finest hour;

111

lies ruined in his pride, cast like a stone.

I'm living
in a world of pure disdain
where every actor lands distress
upon these shores of sanctity.
I close the gate
and all I do is cower
denying every failure I should own.

I'm falling
like a supernatural rain
that floods the land with no quiesce.
I'm searching for eternity.
It seems too late,
but in a world turned sour
there is a field where seeds of hope are sown.

I'm dancing
on a higher plane
where larks and angels coalesce,
cavorting in their jubilee.
We celebrate
the purest healing power
that courses from a golden ancient throne.

February
Andy Allen

When the Reveille sounds in a matt black morning
And cars hiss along wet roads
When commuters cower under driving rain
And travel in dreary silence
A defeated sun retires before you leave work
And the evening's spent in feeble lamplight,
trying to stay warm.

Then, you know it's February.

ideologies
Matt Elmore

must we acknowledge intolerant positions
to follow intent followers avoiding concessions
a schism of fission superseding bipolarism
a religion of prison devoid of precision
liberal conservative radical anachronism
devoid of unity or community only derision
division incision of razored prohibition
invisible individuals devoid of vision
socialistic fizzing cup crippled bedridden
capitalist rationalist nationalist pigeoned
rust on the cusp of impossible coalitions
branded reprimanded for martyred seditions
magnified ratified fried chicken in a prism
fundamental pacifism a sunken anachronism
feminist multiculturalist fending off rhythms
beat to dastardly drums of long dead systems
instamatic autocratic illusionist magician
invoke solutions to solve impossible conditions
transcend flighty ideologies bent on attrition
accept experience and reason in all decisions

Rippling Divinity
Charlene Phare

Solid water hard as stone
Receptors to life's referrals
One splash can't react alone
To make ever decreasing circles

Particles split from their atom
Spirals release, setting them free
Subconscious thoughts, status phantoms
Causing rippling divinity

Within a Cathedral's Silence

Gavin Prinsloo

Words echo with a hollow resonance within a vaulted dome, echoing silence neither heard nor seen, a sepulchral infusion of dream and conscious thought, coursing through a treacle— like medium, sluggish and without form.

Diaphanous hands reach through the entombing stone, reaching and clasping thin air, the needs of the past, present and future feeling the existence of the words vibrating and sliding thickly through the air, yet they are not yet able to ensnare and grasp their meaning within the deafening silence.

Stained glass windows shimmer with an effervescence as light meets obstructions not yet visible to the eye, bending impossible words into prisms that slide gently, slowly in the crevices between granite stones, the mortar between them liquid and slowly sliding; now the only sound to be heard is the grinding of stone upon stone for ears that perceive their existence.

Whispered words are heard among the tectonic rumble as the monolithic pillars shift and change shape and form, recreating themselves, the dome above sliding into the heights of impossibility and the painted frescos change colour and scenes change; paint, ink and mortar oozing into its own form of expression.

The silent cacophony of grinding stone and shifting foundations reaches its crescendo, but there is no need for sound; for obsidian letters form within the screams of the silent birth, giving life to the Word, and form to thought.

Twirling Motion

Karin J. Hobson

Swoosh of dress
Hand pressed
To deep blue skies;
Spinning round and round;
Sufi takes to awake
Universes found.

Sun light to moon at nite,
He does not know;
For, to touch stars
Travel far on ether's tide.

By gallop or trot not;
Twirling motion instead;
Leads one on even score
Of opening door.

Path a walk, but spin talks;
Words to song relay,
Secrets of Heaven's Gate,
And, what may lay beyond.

No trophy to be had
Satisfaction your claim,
Step thru door frame
And, announce your name,
I.
Blessings!

Ephemeral Love

Brandon Adam Haven

Drowning in the shrouds
Of your ephemeral love
Deep humanity is shaken
A plummeted heart forsaken

I bleed ardent tears
Sacrificed in hidden years
Deep into glowing ether
Where dalliance reigns forever

Infatuation is no more
My heart somberly floored
Disparity with no rest
A dissonance of death

Wonders of Life

James Elliot Tully

This journey is to grow and learn.
Allowing these verses to flow
Building a stronger character
To lead others out of the storms of life
With all these verses for all to read
All these wonders running wild
God is the only one with all the answers
He may know the answers
At times feeling it's a waste of breath
Just wanting to touch souls
With words of wonder
At times a deep sadness
Other times endless joy
Oh how many storms I have seen
Learning from each storm
Must remember every pass
Builds strength with a touch of grit
To carry on this long journey called life

Hound Me Down the Highway

Steve Heins

The blackbirds write a warning of wings
Across the colored parchment western sky.
Clouds hide a hellish red sunset.

A southbound semi snarls and spits
pipes full of smoke:
As it pursues me and pulls even,
its windows look fierce
And big eyed like an African mask.
Then it passes me
making its tribal rattle.

Escaping the tug of truck draft,
I slow down behind a church van,
pregnant with parishioners.
The iridescent letters on the back door
glow 'God is so good.'

Into the dusk-ending night,
the van drives without headlights,
like any act of faith.
Finally, I pass the church van
without headlights. I look back
and the van has disappeared:
In its place are the last images of the day:

The script of blackbirds,
the African mask of semis,
and the faithful church van reappear,
until a one-eyed car
sneaks into my rear view mirror.

Looking eye-patched
and sinister in the darkness,
it hounds me down the highway.

Love Twist

Alex Muriuki

Do you know what hurt me most
I thought you were loyal
Oh what a betrayal
Sitting on our bed
Thinking of what happened

Trying to be calm
Refreshing this memory
Haunting moment
Battles in my mind
With answers hard to find

Converging lens of thought
Ruling all I sought
Appreciating time
With more to learn in this game
For life is never same
Thus never will I blame

You left me in the dark
Waiting for the new dawn
Situation caused sadness
With all the loneliness
Still have this hope
The ray of light will shine
Illuminating this life

For my conscious is now clear
Having wiped my tears
With struggle and strive
With twists and turns
With seasons and reasons
Still standing tall
Deep rooted in serenity
No matter the love twist.

Planet for Rent

Paul Holroyd

There's a planet going cheap if you want a fixer-upper,
read carefully through the details while you're sipping
on your cuppa
It's in the solar system deep inside the Milky Way,
third one from the Sun and it's available today

It needs a lot of work, it's been left in such a state,
the previous tenants bled it dry, I don't exaggerate,
they were a bunch of selfish parasites who took and never gave,
until they took too much and now they've taken to their graves

They acted like they owned the place instead of only renting,
even threatened with eviction still there wasn't much relenting.
They had a lifetime contract which made them think
they wrote the rules,
but they broke the ones that mattered, now they're dead,
the stupid fools

If you're taking on this tenancy you'll need to fix the plumbing,
the water level's got too high and tidal waves keep coming,
the wind and Sun are suitable to give you all your power
and please repair the ozone layer, it worsens by the hour

We'll need to check your references before you are considered,
please note it's not just you, we vet all applications delivered.
We're making sure this world will finally be in safer hands,
we have to know you're somebody who truly understands

It comes with sitting tenants whose survival is essential,
so if you care about all life that makes you preferential,
we can't afford more occupants as callous as the last,
if you prove to be you'll be evicted very fast

Apply now if you're suitable and have the right credentials,
send us all your details and show us your potential.
Just one more thing, *you will not be considered* if we're seeing
that you're in any way related to another human being!

Light with Nite
Karin J. Hobson

Your very essence flourishes within my mind;
Immersed in knowing your soul is forever here;
And, though your arm refuses my waist, I know,
Tis still, of ecstasy's coming arrival to undergo;

Oh, 'morrow, over the hill past the moon;
Where you follow the stars to the black hole;
And, there tucked away waiting is our tomorrow;
Oh, tomorrow where warm winds await to embrace;

Where stars shall hum their twinkles,
Moon's wrinkles shall slowly decrease,
The earth a distance no longer in light,
Will dissipate completely from sight.

And, with our omnipresent senses awakened,
And, our dominance to be, together engaged,
Let no man put us under so futile would it be,
They would blanket their eternal light with nite.

The Curse
Jon Wright

Born of blooded tears
Mind broken by invisible spears
Shaped by murderous intent
As my dreams become undreamt

Taken in a fit of rage
Soul pulled from its cage
Anger fills the room like blood
As soul flowed like a flood

The candle flickers no more
No more the waves wash the shore
The song in its final verse
Too late, for is born the curse.

Neurosis
Imelda Zapata Garcia

it slipped quietly down the rabbit hole
this ever present crowded essence
while I bled through every scroll
pouring into body and soul
each step taken of my presence

all at once a melding took place
lost in translation of each endeavor
down the spiral slow descent
went in fragments every trace
losing sense while thinking clever

cadence tripped with yearning passion
fought to keep a clear perspective
through the struggle of the ages
torn up pages, mind in session
slipping past, though not elective

The Blue Between
You and Me
Michael Balner

As high as stars on
a clear summer night,
As deep as dreams found
in your eyes,
As warm as oceans'
tidal waves,
As chill as knowing that
it all will end
is the blue
between
you and me
and you

Stardust

Larry Bracey

Don't look away,
You're going to miss it all,
You're supposed to make a wish,
If you see one fall,

Millions upon millions,
Of little balls of light,
Decorating the sky,
Bringing the day to night,

Stories about what they are,
Theories we've all heard,
Some make perfect sense,
While others are just absurd,

The one I like to believe,
Is that we are the stars in the sky,
That flew to the heavens,
The moment we die,

And when the sky is full,
We are given another chance,
Falling back to earth,
As you watch our beautiful dance,

And should there be a trail,
Left as we leave the night,
That's when you say the words,
Starlight, Starbright.

My Personal Snow Globe

Tom Watkins

I went to greet the snow
It was falling
and calling for me

I could have slipped on
my cross-country skis,
but I decided to walk
and not glide

The meteorologist made
an accumulation promise
Walking with snow
is good for the soul
It cleanses the mind
to be surrounded by softness

I purposely take short steps
even shuffle for stability
My cold hands
are out of my pockets
always prepared
for a great fall
When I do, the snow crystals
cradle me

Stop and listen
to the snowflakes collide
as they drift down
accumulating on the ground
Building up depth on the trees
as my feet make
a joyful crunching sound

The snow falls like a whisper
The quietness of white abounds
The crunch of my feet
The rhythmic patter of my heart

The crystals building
on the evergreens
The sparkle of the flakes
as they lay neatly on the ground
The ducks waddle
and paddle in the lake
seemingly enjoying the snowflakes with me

The trees take on skeletal features
The snow clings to every branch
The wind unveils a mighty mast
as the trees wave a welcome
to me on my walk

Much in life does not sink in
As my boots leave
an impression of where I have been
A clear white palate lies before me
I note a deer was here before me

I stop and listen
to the white quiet
I am stepping where no one
has stepped before
The white noise being
clarity of what is before me

Why not leave a childhood mark
of my winter existence
A snow angel to tag the spot
All is right in this magical world

I have entered my own
human snow globe
Nothing better
than a soft quiet listen
I stop and give thanks
for those I love

stalk and pounce

Matt Elmore

mine eyes
shine no mercy
for there is no light
I am obfuscated carnal
in this world
of bloodiest night

devoid of patience
relations or sin
only wild urges
drive me within

words like claws
dig most deep
into oblivious veins
stalking slow and steady
fang ever ready
until only a carcass remains

feasting on doubt
hungry for need
this world is mine
on fragile fear I feed

unrepentant discontent
salacious animal soul
silently retreating
return repeating
an attack to swallow
all helpless whole

Deserted
Gregory Richard Barden

step ...

across the sill
this haunted house
walls of torn paper, dripping
crumbling plaster ceilings
hanging like rotten vines on this
bony frame
dark, broken windows, the
empty eyes that stare
once aglow with
the bright from within
life and light ... and love
made a home
until ...
just an ember —
one flame of your kiss —
and it was gutted
burned raw and ruined
with no thought to what filled these rooms
or graced the facades
or warmed the meager marrow ...
now all phantoms
howling in the barren halls
sodden and saddened
for sake of the abandoned —
the threadbare —
dilapidated ... desolate
welcome to the
vacancy ...
your fool.

Troubles

Terry Bridges

I am aghast, penitent at heart
Sand sifts my pain into a desert
No refreshing rain to wash me clean
Dry bones a skeleton that creaks with age

The rattle of death swallowed a bitter taste
But the quiet moon keeps me alive
I will not forfeit my existence lightly
While it shines its luminescence saves me

There's more to heaven and earth that anybody knows
Mysteries burst in my heart like stars
The black sky like liquorice night advances
I compose this in silence and wait

Coda. I wrote this straight off onto my phone.
See what you think.

Terrible Triumph

Steve Wheeler

When it's win or lose, at all costs win
A dirty foul, a surreptitious grin
A sliding tackle in the sucking mud
Studs up to rake and draw the blood
Deep in the heat and thunder of the game
Triumph and defeat can both be blamed
For dredging up a multitude of sin
When it's win or lose, at all costs win

Don't ask an ant
if he can or he can't

Eric Aguilar

Ask the soda in a can
if an ant
can or he can't.
Strength in teamwork
when it doesn't
look like they can.
Ants sink in shifting sand,
but, don't ask an ant
if it can or it can't.
It won't answer
It would rather
do this and that
than gab or chat.
Oh, but...
don't ask two ants
who can or who can't.
It is equivalent to ask'n
if Ali could jab.
Faster than they can
fight each other,
they wrestle and grab
and even form a link
to pull the ant that can't back —
so don't ask if two ants
can or they can't.
They scout, collect,
retrieve and process;
stored now
for when they can't.
They communicate and
even laugh and rant.
They master plan.
So, don't ask an ant
if it can or it can't.

Where Am I?

Geoff Edwards

If cheaters never lie and
Liars never cheat

Where am I?

If Rembrandt burns his brush and
Our Love was just a rush

Where am I?

If an apple is not shined and
My words were so unkind

Where am I?

Continue the brush stroke
Glisten the fruit
Demolishing the hurt
Can you, are you able?

The words I said were vain
The words I spoke were unwise
My double-sided tongue
Cut me, with the look in your eyes.

Where am I?

the revelation
Jan Kenneth Velle

i cried yesterday
for the things i couldn't play
echoes of night...
in my humble dreams
my heart goes on and on
every hungry heart
is finding themself in art
i call on your last meeting
with the ones who want to be
i am sure we all come between
cosmic colours rest in sunlight
endless forgiving shades...
takes every burden free
just the way i wanted to be
love-song's stains in my mind
just like attempts for restless forgiveness
i am in a quiet substance
right now in my love
that chases all of us

A Face as Beautiful as Hers
Quint Essential

She often spits out words at me
sharper than a knife
spoken with all honestly
she's cut me more than twice
then she wants to kiss the bruise
it seems to grant me grace
scares my flesh and bone to think
that evil shares a face
as beautiful as hers

Apathy in Love

Lora Lee

In the beginning of our love,
she never dared to soar,
Her heart, it just couldn't venture,
upon that particular shore.
She clung to me with apathy,
a lukewarm embrace,
For love was just a fallacy,
in our cold and empty space.
Her eyes conveyed a subtle plea,
a longing to be free,
Yet bound by chains of empathy,
she stayed in love with me.
In moments of silence,
I'd wonder where she roamed,
Her eyes staring
far away,
in distant lands unknown.
Her laughter,
once a symphony,
A sound oh so sweet,
Turned into a hollow chime,
as our love faced its defeat.
The day I chose to set her free,
our story's final verse,
She hid a sigh of sweet relief
behind her somber curse.
Her eyes, once veiled in shadows,
now danced with happiness and light,
For in the end,
my love's release,
had given her love flight.

Look Back Without Anger
Russell Jacklin

Darker moments, when shadows fall,
When wrong is done, by one, to all,
A gentle thought to bear in mind,
This sentiment, so wise, so kind.
Whenever someone's deeds offend,
Consider first which path they wend,
When good and evil hearts collide,
What notions, and what motives hide?
For in that understanding gaze,
A Pharos shines in murky haze.
Instead of rage or deep dismay,
Light emerges and guides our way.
For every action has a cause,
A virtuous tale of flaws, and flaws,
The seeds of empathy shall sow
Where prejudice was quick to grow.
The choices made, the path we tread,
May stem from hurt, our fears, or dread,
By seeking truth, we start to find,
Fragile essence of humankind.
No longer bound by anger's might,
We learn to see in softer light,
A chance to heal, to bridge the strife,
Reclaim the beauty of this life.
So, let compassion be our guide,
In moments when those hearts collide,
For understanding may transcend,
The pain inflicted wounds that mend.
Transgressed, one against another,
Look past the surface, deep discover,
How can evil deeds be thwarted,
Compassionate perception flaunted.

Aroma
Cheena Puri

The escapades for savouring
the aroma of freedom,
Amidst life's unexplainable twists,
Moments which were the only means to be oneself—
and breathe life.

The precious moments snatched from the barred existence ;
The peals of laughter as the purity of pearls,
The joy of freedom as the sky full of birds,
The warmth of love and togetherness,
As the brightness of the sun.

To grab the fresh breath of life...
To fly with the refreshing cool breeze,
To savour the aroma brewing from the essence of
one's true, free being.

Shelter
Fouzia Sheikh

I'll give you shelter
from the pouring rain
An unknown swelter
Being mixed with pain.

My shelter will help you hide
stay here to escape your home
Trust us to be your life's guide
Safety for wherever you roam.

But our shelter won't last
like all things
stuck in the past.

Sad Thoughts
Praise Edwin

We've gathered at the campsite
to listen to the trembling fire's voice
that speaks to us only at night,
in a solemn tone void of noise:
its crackling sound makes us lost in thought,
over things we've sold or things we've bought;
our lives seemed like a stream of purchases
done countless times and in multiple places.
Yet we still haven't bought anything worthwhile
except things so dark, sinister and viciously vile!

We've gathered at the campsite
to listen to the trembling fire's voice:
when the Moon shines its white light,
while our frigid souls are void of will or choice;
We've done all our works to fulfil our course,
yet in them we find no joy only regrets and remorse.
The Nightingale comes gently to sober with us,
its solemn sound tune affecting our lost subconscious;
what do we call 'love' and what do we term as 'hate'
when both are served simultaneously on the same plate?

We've gathered at the campsite
to listen to the trembling fire's voice:
the heavens takes pity on us for our plight
but those in hell with celebrations they rejoice;
the sky is now a dark bluish midnight powdered ash,
and shooting stars had begun to mysteriously flash
over our heads like they were all in a big fat rat race
though we took no notice; lost through time and space.
We wandered back to things that was long gone,
those things we thought would forever go undone!

Colour Me
Lorna MacLaren

Colour me blue when I'm feeling down,
my eyes are empty and my mouth's upside down.
Colour me red when I grimace
with frustration and anger, trying to keep it in place.
Colour me yellow when I'm feeling calm
with no thought in my head to cause me alarm.
Colour me purple when magic is in the air,
I'll become creative, try to do it with flair.
Colour me green when I'm connecting with nature,
living and breathing all its beauty and flavour.
Colour me rainbow, let my spirit fly free
as that is the time I really feel me.
Shade me in black when I'm dead and gone
for all colour has faded and can't be redrawn.
Cast me as empty, now merely a husk
soon to become nothing, turned into dust.
So colour me now while I'm still here on earth
and show me that my life does have some worth.

Colour me

It Could be You
Susan Ila Davis

I have a name, it's someone that I use to be.
Now I am homeless, and no one will remember me.
I had a face, it was pretty and clean.
Now I look so old, and sometimes I feel so mean.
People stare, or ignore me like I don't exist.
I just smile, and try to hide my dirty fist.
I was like them once. Sorrow didn't know my name.
Sorrow is my bed now, I see that we are all the same.

The Longest Night
Lorna McLaren

The longest night, twenty first of December,
still wondering, still waiting, still being a pretender.
The longest night with no-one to hold,
looking for answers, feeling so cold.
The longest night, I wish it was over,
so tired of pretending I'm with my lover.
The longest night, I can't cry any more,
Tomorrow's a new day, a day I'll ignore.
What lies ahead? I have nothing in sight,
I just have to get through the longest night.

Chronicles of the Here and Now
Archie Papa

I am not the past
all but forgotten and lost
for sorrow somehow remembered
and teardrops bearing the cost

I am not the future
brought on a wish and a prayer
as fear will complicate hatred
love will simplify care

I am only this moment
everything all in one place
details of spending or saving
drawn whichever the case

I am the here and now
wisdom in reason and rhyme
and we shall forever remain
together somewhere in time

Here
Deborah Griffin Howard

feeling like invisible ink
hoping for someone
to erase me
or make me
visible again
I am ready to fight
to be alive
for
I am living in a shadow
of death inside
wherever you are
just look my way
and feel me
feel my pain
for here
it hurts
to be alive

The Apple
Gavin Prinsloo

Ah said he, this apple has no tree!
Aye said she, now come and play with me!
Just take a bite, said she to the he,
Just a nibble it will set you free!
On the eve of our lives the apple will glow,
Said she to the he, all the things you will know!
He looked at the she and gave into their sin
Eden deleted from their recycle bin

My Soul's Communion with Nature

Cheena Puri

In silence are they heard —
Dancing winds, laughing clouds
Chirping birds all sing aloud.
There is a communion of my soul with Nature's soul.
Strolling on the trail alone
Under the canopy of tall trees ten-fold.
Golden sunlight gushing through the leaves
Embracing you in its warmth and glee.

You are no more on your own
As Nature surrounds you three-fold.
Gazing at the deep blue sky,
Which slowly absorbs you in its depth
And swirls you afloat in its vastness.

Look yonder where the ancient mountain range
Rests since eons in its complacent phase,
Like a gigantic well-fed and sedate.

There is mystery in the holes carved eerily on the trees
You wonder what all is hidden in the deep.
The upturned-roots wind and wind as meandering snakes,
Engulfing the broad trunk up till its length,
And underneath, the agile squirrels play and peck on food,
Inviting you to meditate on
Nature's strange and silent pace.

Nature's soul communes with mine
As it uplifts and swings me in its windy arms,
My soul too responds to nature's sounds
And leaps out unto the sky
And experiences a momentous joy!

Arsenic and Rhetoric

Gavin Prinsloo

Clogged lungs and rancid skies,
worlds apart from marble floors,
Opulence and wealth abound,
strengthened by bloody wars

Arsenic and rhetoric cloud the senses,
and turn the world to dust,
Framed and torn the skin of life,
from the mantle to the crust

Ages past and change is due,
but not in Nature's plan,
For change is what *we* created,
and the flames of change we fan

Words bereft of logic will be carried
upon the smoke and dust,
For logic is as greed does,
for greed and wealth a lust

As dirt is piled for plunder,
and oil lubricates the will of man's endeavour,
The change is due in the course of fact,
extinction is a change forever

There is no hope in rhetoric,
for words cannot stem the tide of death,
For every stone unturned
in search of immortal wealth,
robs a tree of our mortal breath

Forgotten

Graeme Stokes

He sits broken amidst his shattered hopes,
the pavement his cold mistress
The red neon lights a flashing strobe,
as his heart bleeds torn and listless

The passers-by a kinetic forest, a horde of hostile legs
Normality goads a cacophonous chorus,
his sanity dwells on the edge

He steps outside himself, a desolate plea,
in a doleful monotone
A barely audible 'any change please?'
conviction a long way from home!

Hot shame scolds his freezing core, lacerates his every fibre
His pride plummets to the obdurate floor, survival his only driver

It wasn't always this way! A mournful reflect,
as fleeting coin embraces cup
Then economic non viability set,
and addiction became his crutch!

Accusing glares cut deep in his soul,
castrating his clinical world
Sunken eyes alert on stray boot patrol,
dilate for projectiles hurled!

In the sodden cardboard that forms his nest,
he longs for a word in his ear
The 'hungry please help!' cries an SOS,
rains down in black ink tears!

With renewed focus he tries to engage,
a coffee from a kindly stranger
It's not just from pockets he longs for change,
as fight and resolve grows fainter

He gazes at the consoling stars, optimistic, wild and free
Faith waning, he begins to pray hard,
'Dear God please don't forsake me!'

South

Andy Allen

Skyscrapers
Billboards
Obliterated sky
And never a birdsong is heard.
Interminable traffic
Pressed through old narrow lanes.
Construction
Destruction
A cacophony of action.
Bangkok sucks you in
and spits out your remains.

Like breaching a weir,
The highway spreads
And traffic freely flows.
Skies open
Birds sing
And the radio plays my favourite songs.
Green paddies shimmer
Between full rivers
And the distant shadow
Of spiky limestone mountains
Promises nature's glory.

And now time passes slowly
Between the mountains and the sea
Low rise
High tide
Smiling faces
Open spaces.
Absorb the sky
Hear the birds
Let the sea winds
Blow the city from your hair.

People Power

Crispulo Tapa

What's this hubris all about,
that history can repeat itself?
Old faces, familiar voices,
chanting similar verses
The curse they heap on this
despot and his loved ones
Unforgiveness their battle-cry,
a fallacy of dubious intent.

The rumblings of the
privileged class,
Drowning the wails
of the downtrodden.
Their chatter reminiscent
of a revolution past
Where they toppled
and banished a despot.

A deranged old man rings
the bells long silent.
Its hollow frame bellowing,
splitting our eardrums.

He tolls the bells again;

for the Church gone blind

for the politicians gone wild;

for the drug lords gone crazy;

for the elite and greedy;

for the woke, careless and free.

The hungry wolves reawaken,
avengers of lost influence

The symbol they built of
people power is gone,
Its pretences exposed,
devoid of altruistic intent.

Is this what our heroes
died for?

Hungry citizens go around town

Scrounging for McDonald
chicken scrap

While priests feast
on offerings for the King.

Let the bells be tolled again, and
wake us up from deep slumber
Let the bells ring long and real loud,
and break the apathy within us.

The Falcon on the Edge

Aaron Blackie

The falcon lost
Its viscerally propelled voice,
Awakened to my
Slumbered staggering
By the windowpane—

A call at the dews of mornings,
Wakefield stretched on
The dreamy eyes fermented
For the solitude beckoning...

I have fallen into hazy
Season that caged my days,
To wheeled around shadows

Weighty on my soul;

Rhythms gyrating before
Flabby tongues,
In the currents of muddy curiosity...
The wears of the spirit's
Bond to the season of anomy...

The falcon cackled
On the pole of intimacy like
The familiar cock crow at dawn...
Bravery at the liveliness
Of its serration calls, preened
On my tickling eardrums:

Awake to the random
Wings of the
Curious dews, early
To beckons on
Musing onto vibes,
At life's tenderly tended
Hours never to be
For ever recapped again...

My soul yet slogged it out;
Slumbering sleepy foam,
Rested on the soothing
Depth of snoring,
Avid to chained me caged
Against the clarion call,
To creative wakefulness...

Then mystery rend my
Springy soul apart...

The keen eyes of the resilient
Falcon pierced through
My dream's streaming,

Soaring through the
Stilled water of my inwardness,
A sonorous song:
The early riser, dictates the pace,
Before the evening swaps...Oh
Incongruent sleeper...

Awakened!
I am rebirth to the strands
Of my glow, in solitude's curious roads,

Again to behold life's sunny side...

Unwritten
Jon Wright

We are unfinished tales
Tipping on the edge of life's scales
Hanging from the edge
Falling from the sky

We are the broken dreams
The unfinished schemes
The rise of the sun
And the fall of the moon

We are the ones taken too soon
The unfinished book
The untold tale
The unsung song

We are the ones that never were
The shadows in the light
The one's death has bitten
We are the unwritten

Those Bloody Wheels (Sin)

Paul Rogers

Seven fifty seven, then eight twenty five
and every each hour until dusk.
When the doors never close and the boundaries
of time ever widen as anything goes.
So I stand there in line with my partners in crime
and a song that I've yet to compose
And the wheels on the bus go around they go round
and the wheels on the bus they go round.

There's no step to climb, but once I'm on board
there's a surge towards each empty seat.
But I stand with my doubt 'case there's still some way
out to prevent my inevitable defeat.
Then the wheels on the bus they go round they go round
yes the wheels on the bus still go round.
"Sit here next to me" said the man in the suit
as the lady in red shared a smile.

The wig and the gown looked at me
with a frown and his finger ticked off the next mile.
Still the wheels on the bus they go round they go round
yes those wheels they go round they go round.

I stare ashen faced in the direction I faced,
looking back bought regret and some pain,
And the long road ahead bore the tears
I had shed and the lost simply hid from the rain.
Yes the wheels on the bus just went round
as before yes the wheels went around they went round.

Vacant seats occupied so I cling to my rail,
hesitation and fear take their grip,
I look back once again, from this desolate train
wondering why I'd bought into this trip.
And the wheels still went round like before they go round,
just the same yes around and around.

As each station goes by there's no way to get off
and the wheels scream inside of my head
The scars never heal and the track guides each wheel
 into flesh and the blood it is bled...
To those wheels that go round, bloody wheels they go round
yes the wheels still turn round and around.

Should I wait for a stop can I break from this chain,
or simply let go of my past,
'Cause the road I now seek with the fools
and the weak bring new pleasures that can never last.

When will this ride end, when can I descend
I'll not wait for this trip to expire,
For the freedom He gave and the love
that He shows gives me strength to escape from the fire.

So I'll just take my very own leap of blind faith,
then my feet find their way to a door,
Still the wheels turned around and round
but I've learned what is truth, not uncertain but sure.

Still the wheels they go round
on that same crimson ground,
but I'm not on board I broke free,

I've got rid of the load,
still I walk my long road
not alone
'cause He's walking with me.

Ruby Suffused Cochineal Human

Hahona Pita Batt

Bone soaked summer sentinels
insipiently mollified
neath cumulae embosomed vistas
Barbiturate engorged
vermilion runes
wallowing in chimera swill.

Decaffeinated voices echo
as lethargy inculcates
tacit compunction
Notions of hallow-less grace
questions doused in saline inoculate
Notions of truth in beggared belief
where have all the answers gone?

Flora gently weeps
pistil whipping bipartisan fauna
Cut out gargoyle clones
pollinated neath aerosol verbose
Binomial nomenclature
classified dereliction.

Ruby suffused cochineal humans
basted whole in Solaris contrive
Circumspect greyscale nomads
Directionless deflated decorations
drenched in eunuch pleurisy.

Politically corrected rhetorical vaccinate
Human race pinioned taut
in phat cat sanctioned decree
Napoleonic wagers
vetoed in watershed abdicate
Wellington's Waterloo
symbolic synonymous symposium.

War and peace symbiosis

in acute catalepsy
And yet while laurel sofas avail rest
the beast goes to work
Marking the tempo in
barcode inseminate
humanity left to ponder
Diablo's 666 machinate.

Crystal Chandeliers
Charlene Phare

We're crystal chandeliers
Suspended from the skies
When we feel the darkness
Heaven hears our cries
We have fallen from the ceiling
Shattered across the earth
But we're crystal chandeliers
We shine for all we're worth

We are fragile fragments
Broken by fleeting looks
Developed over time
More delicate than books
We have the ability
To glow with all our might
Add a touch of glamour
Lasting longer than the night

If you put down your whiskey
I will write you a poem
Weave my words with droplets
Guidance forever flowing
Treat yourself with care
Don't become shards of glass
We're crystal chandeliers
With added sparkle and class

Nyctophile
Lorna McLaren

She walks into the night's embrace,
feels the air caress her face,
the moon smiles down, glows in the sky,
she sees the stars, breathes out a sigh.
In the silence there she stands
with upturned face and outstretched hands
in trancelike state, she seems to be
lost in her own reality.
Child of the night she spurns the day
as dark becomes her time for play,
a nyctophile is what she is,
unto the night herself she gives.
In solitude she is set free,
such beauty there for her to see,
then as the night's reclaimed by dawn
just like the morning mist she's gone.

would you be mine?
Matt Elmore

if I were to fashion stars into a cloak
would you model it for me to invoke
the infinite pleasures of which I seek
my love my heart my soul to keep…
if I could capture the lions roar
or encage courage of which to implore
of wildness from your smile divine
your kiss your touch would you be mine…?
if I could name just one thing
one book one choice one song to sing
i would forever ask you to be mine
now and tomorrow unto the end of time

You Belong to Yesterday

Lianne Neeson

Sometime between last night and tomorrow morning
In those moments when even the air holds it breath
The colour drains from the world
waiting to be painted in a new palette
Those times when the spiders feel safe
to weave their webs and catch the dew
I almost hear your voice
Just a feeling of a word
Brushing past my fingertips
Sometime when the sleeping are not even dreaming
As the clocks stop ticking because
there's no one to hear them
The world is frozen for a moment
between reality and where I want to be
I nearly see your face
Just a glimpse of movement
Whispering to me
Then the illusion is shattered
The earth spins into the never ending tomorrows
and you belong to yesterday.

Day Lilies

Susan Ila Davis

Three years she had hid in the gloom of shade
Not seeking glory, her existence to fade

Moved to the sunlight, away from the dark
Now she blooms between spaces , her colors stark

The Bees celebrate the birthing of blooms
Gleaming Day Lilies will find sleep with the moon.

In the Beginning
Michael Balner

In the beginning, there was an end,
there was darkness and then,
the sun gave birth to a new day.

The heart stopped dead,
the lies were unclad,
and self-deception
lost its ground.
The fierce fires
devoured land and
vomited smoke and ash
that gave birth to a carpet
of emerald green grass. The
heart picked the beat again.

In the beginning, there is an end
the wounds of old
are now reopened
so they can be healed once for all.

Midsummer Glow
Joseph Andrew Miller

The flames leap and flick
Through warmed conversation.
Friends and their fabled foibles,
Sparks drifting in lazy sweet smoke
On a soft summer-night breeze.

A roaring past feeds
A smouldering present
Till embers ebb and ripple, painted
As a late sunset glow, dancing
With the yester-light of tomorrow.

the cheat of a wordless poet
Matt Elmore

lovely lunar lamp; light my way
in ghostly splendor, glaze the night
with deathly pallor, colorless in grey
shine your most helpless light
high in the sky, to fade my heart
tearing my every sense apart

for upon a very scene as this
my every dream chokes; even now
I near the brook my love did kiss
to invoke a most solemn vow;
that all my life I would profess
to provide for her loveliness

yet even a poet could not supply
words for that moment of duress
which cruel endeavor did supply
the cheat which did my love undress
or how i now curse that ghastly moon
that stole my love away too soon

Night
Lorna McLaren

The night it came so swiftly down
in lurid technicolour gown,
so unashamed left hanging there,
like a wanton thing laid bare.
Then cloaked in black to cover sin
enveloping it all within,
blanketing us from its shame
'til morning's modesty's reclaimed.

Fade to Grey
Hahona Pita Batt

I wish
I was
a lemon tree
or even
a pebble
on a beach
innocently cajoled
to flow
with the motion
of existence.
But...
in the end
everything
and everyone
goes away
into the
cavernous abyss
of oblivion.
Feeble
frail
fraught
thought
and notion
fermentation
forbodes
a desolate
vestibule vacuum
into a genesis
of tabula rasa...
square one
empty slate.
Now where
shall we begin
before
the easel
paint dries?

Alchemy

Sharon Toner

Wanting to know and yet not

Trying to stop that train of thought
The one that runs away with itself
At a hundred miles an hour
That very thought you wish
Time would rapidly devour
It's like pleasure and pain
Sandwiched between
That hedonistic desire
Yet you're trying to put out the fire
Heart pounding and pulse racing
Thoughts you keep trying to denounce
As the clock ticks louder
Like the residue of smoking gunpowder
Focusses all of your attention
Creating that inevitable apprehension

Wanting to know and yet not

You ignite your train of thought
Till the rush sweeps you along
As you lose yourself in the song
Immersed deep within the melody
Trying to find its integrity
Allowing each second its moment to be
Attempting to understand the code for alchemy
Willing to accept that everything changes with time
Even if only a microscopic enzyme
One that the eye cannot see
Whilst still searching for life's psychic key
Your mind ignited and stirred
Like a lion completely undeterred
Roaming around in its lure
Until the moment it's shot
Wanting to know and yet not.

Adagio in G Minor
Imelda Zapata Garcia

Adoration brings me such sorrow
Deafening cries flood every morrow
Anxiously, I search for forlorn passion
Grinding the stone, of my hearts fashion
Injured, it hardened to harkening summons
Opulent dreams, fade slowly to common

Inching away, the tender perception
Naught, is of value, love's no exception

Garish, grotesque
the wound, forged by deception

Minor compensation, offered by sacrifice
Inconceivable grief, grips, lost paradise
Nevertheless, a soul strives for revival
Optimizing the gravity of love, for survival
Rewarding the struggle, with blessings
unrivalled

Death
Tracey Louise Brunning

Death slinks around,
wafting cheeks like soft chiffon,
ruffling downy hairs,
as it creeps up our spines,
whispering secrets
in the pink flesh of ears,
flushing faces with memories,
tinged clear in our minds.

Death strokes our busy recollections

Selfie Queen

Lorna McLaren

She strikes a pose,
the shutter clicks,
another pic, another fix,
her need to be out on display,
what is it makes her feel this way?

She counts the likes,
the loves, the cares,
waits for the comments
and the shares,
the more she gets
the more she craves,
at her own beauty
she's quite amazed.

A self-indulgent selfie queen
adding to her self-esteem.
One day her followers will stray
to another beauty on display,
when they go and all is lost
leaves me wondering at what cost,
re-joining the ranks of the unknown
a selfie queen without her throne.
with its calloused fingers,
ready to pull up the blanket
and tuck us up forever
in the bosom of Earth's cradle,
to be lulled for eternity
by the breath of life...

The End of Days

Archie Papa

Onward the journey til the end of days
bridges and paths intersect in their maze
time drives the engine, never been late
and through the abyss we navigate

Over the hills to the other side
forward momentum gains our stride
everything true is clearly in sight
past shadows of doubt cast in its light

Forever is waiting for never to begin
with an honest lie and a faithful sin
sorrow will labor while laughter plays
onward the journey til the end of days

Motionless

Joe Callanan

Suddenly it's cold
I'm doing as I'm told
I want to grow old

I have a colourless coat
In elections I don't bother to vote
I don't like how winners always gloat

I'm not going out of my way
No-one is interested in what I have to say
I got too much going on today

I wish things could be better
I'll try to focus on pleasure
But I'm not a real go getter

I didn't think life was this fast
My life is now part of the past
I wish I could make it last

My friends want to see change
I'm told they must be strange
I'll allow society to rearrange

I can't engage
In my own rage
Not in this day and age

Suddenly it's cold
I want to grow old
I'm doing as I'm told

I want to get out of here
When I feel the fear
I know when it's near

I won't make a sound
I'll just walk around
Keep low stay underground

I see who is killing who
I can't tell anyone what to do
Even if I wanted to

More blood will spill
Again I feel a cold chill
I've come to a standstill

I'm doing as I'm told
I want to grow old
Suddenly it's cold

My Sweet Delusion

Brandon Adam Haven

Through the depths of my mind
A subconscious world unfolds
Where veracity fades and delusion takes hold
My perception beguiled by a noxious brew
As I plummet within, my fate now in view

The world around me wanes to a monochrome hue
As I'm engulfed by fatal ensnarement
My heart palpitates, my breaths inchoate
As the venom within me reaches its apotheosis state

Phantasms pirouette before my eyes
As I sink into a realm of fallacious guise
A realm where nothing is what it seems
And I'm shackled by my own tattered hopes and dreams

In the deep clutches of this most malevolent fate
I'm weak and powerless to extricate
As the drugs hold sway and drag me down
I become adrift in a world where no hope is found

In the embrace of death, will I find release?
From the agony and the afflictions
and the maladies that cease
But even so, I'm not unbound
As I'm assailed by the reminiscences
of what once was profound

Oh, how I yearn to reverse the hands of time
And undo the missteps that led to my decline
But it's too late now, the harm is done
And I'm left to face the consequences of what I've become

So here I lie like a shattered entity
Trapped in a world of my own private misery
Haunted by the apparition of coldness devised
And consumed by the sweet delusion that took my life

Anchored
Katja Viitamäki

Sun and the moon
eternally bonded by fate
Fire and water
born to burn
and forever sail
on the sea of sorrow
where the ship was anchored...
and left to die....

Heaven and hell
two sides of the same picture
The warmth and the cold
nothing more to tell
when the last sentence are told...

Love and hate
are crucified together
in grief...
Two sides of the same picture
nothing more to sell
when the last leaf
fell
in silence
Born to live
born to die
eternally bonded by fate..

Iodine 1963

Paul Rogers

I can recount but not recall, how my free flight 'came my free fall,
from my push bike at Herons Cross was dumped and hit the road.
My blood bright red though tarmac bled to skin in shreds and my
poor head was spinning freely like a top and out of my control.
The stinging pain, the bloody graze the haze and my malaise grew
worse, as I began to curse and nurse the wounds of my demise.
And though my bike lay prone on ground, the wheels still turned as
round and round, the ringing in my ears now cleared as fog when
sun comes out.

Back to earth again I'm fine, so to my saddle I did climb, bit my
tongue and forced a smile, hummed a song to bring some sense,
'cause I would find no recompense if I was late for work.
Fifteen years and my first job, peddled hard as shoulders throbbed,
past railway sheds with engines Stoked, the Trent flowed on my
back now bent and on to Hanley town.

Up Burslem's hill now five to eight, down the bank to factory gate
at Middle Port on time not late I got there just in time.

And Bill peered down from window's frame, "What you been
playing, silly games?" "Come in," he said and I climbed down, as
he with bottle chocolate brown undid the cap and with a frown he
looked me up and looked me down and shook his balding head.
He sat me up on three legged stool, peeled the skin like some lost
ghoul, my sweat fell free to form the pool in which I hoped to
drown.

This'll kill the germs he cried and to the wounds he did apply the
contents of the bottle I'd observed as I'd walked in.
"Iodine will do the trick", he raised a smile and took the mick, the
pain it pierced me to the quick, I clenched my harrowed face:
Not wanting to admit defeat, I left the stool and to my feet did stand
without a cry or bleat, like lambs bred for the plate.
So to the packing shed at pace to drink some tea with sugar laced
and share the crimson scars that graced my ego 'spite my youth.
Does it sting? the questions came as hobbling like a man now lame,

supporting my poor aching frame, I answered with a nod.
And though at heart my mates were kind, the sympathy was hard
to find so back to pots, the daily grind and butt of endless jokes.
I still remember with a grin, the jokes we told now growing thin, the
boiling pot enamelled tin, nostalgia and the rest.

The sullied cap the gate-man wore, the three-legged stool, the
wooden floor, the subtle whit and words I swore not fit for gentle-
men.

The pottery's on the tele now, new lease of life, sacred cow, as
hopefuls make posh cups and bow, as pride before the fall.
But I enjoy the yesterday, the irony, the verbal play, the things
forgotten, words I say and bright new first-aid box.

Rats
Imelda Zapata Garcia

Toxic creatures of the night
crawling up to blur the white
grimy fingers point from right
claiming theirs, the only sight
Tearing at long held upright
entertainment for all delight
cutting at the heart's insight
just to spread hatred and spite
Rats with mousy filthy blight
sit in sprawling wretched hight
doling out to feverishly incite
a crazed response to thus ignite
a raging, unrelenting plight
within a treasured human right

Words
Donna Rancourt

Random words seeking rhyme
with a cadence, fill my mind
words repeating over time
past and present intertwine.
Perceptions descriptive narrative
arranged in rhythmic eloquence
a better understanding give
portrayal of one's inner sense.

irreprehensible
Matt Elmore

sometimes I resemble
an invisible sadistic
trespassing mortician

aura relic
of my own rebellious
irreprehensible
superstition

embalming embedding
convoluted in repetition
revealing an obnoxious
perilous perdition

selective of souls
failing to mention
our silent triumphs
of rejected contention

claiming tomorrow
for today's apprehension

Ironic
Mary McLeish

Pretty as the picture in the frame
Foundation the base of her natural beauty
Rosy blush of her cheeks
Reflects the gloss of her lips
Fine lines trace the curves of her lids
And shadows highlight the depth of her eyes
A spray of hair kept behind her ears.
She hears the bell. One last check all is well
He opens the door, stands his stick by the wall
Pats his guide-dog and smiles,
He remembers her well.

Look Up
Paul Holroyd

Look up.....
at every rain-drenched cloud, with lightening bright and
thunder loud, the wrath of nature at her worst she orders all
the clouds to burst
The weakest race we run for cover terrified of Nature's mother
as if we'd done her wrong somehow and so she wants to kill
us now

Look up.....
into the deep blue skies where burning sun attacks your eyes
and tries to burn your tender skin, again we have to hide
within
The faded moon will blow a kiss beyond the endless blue
abyss, a reminder that our whole life's worth is but a blink to
Mother Earth

Look up.....

and see the darkest night, a trillion stars are shining bright,
our curiosity running rife imagining all kinds of life
If we could wave a magic wand and reach another world
beyond perhaps we'd see someone like you looking up into
the blue

Look up.....
and see the world around with all its wonders to be found,
mountains, rivers, giant trees, rolling hills and raging seas, all
the plants and living souls acting out their given roles, we're
nothing but a tiny crease in Mother Nature's masterpiece

The Nocturnal Realm
Brandon Adam Haven

The celestial orb has descended far beyond the horizon
And the firmament is adorned with stellar jewels
As the nocturnal veil envelops the land
And the world is shrouded in an ethereal hue

The zephyr whispers through the verdant foliage
As the nocturne creatures stir from their quiet slumber
Their aphonic howls go yet unheard
As they search for souls to plunder

The resplendent moon illuminates the earth
As it casts its opalescent glow upon all below
And the constellations twinkle in the night sky
Like a celestial tapestry woven by the divine

Oh how wondrous is the nocturnal realm
With its enigmatic beauty and mystifying charm
A world of magic and mystery shown
To those who dare to venture into the unknown

Your White Shadow

Mike Absalom

Last night under a huge sky
I stepped outside and peering upwards
saw you float silently past,
in the white and silent shape of an owl,
eyes glittering with moon dust,
seeing me, and not seeing me.

You are a seeded sphere of life
tumbling on the moon's breath,
a silent incantation as you pass me by
casting your white shadow against my black darkness.

I am entranced by the beauty of your form.
Your dandelion clock counts imaginary hours
but each one is registered in a living breath,
as if there is some sense in that childish tally.

And always I am entranced by the beauty of the form.

Last night, under a huge sky
I stepped outside and peering upwards
saw you sail silently past
in the white and threatening shape of an owl,
eyes glittering with moon dust,
seeing me, and seeing me too well.

This morning you are gone, like fingerprints on a river.
It is hard to gather you as evidence.
I have looked for moon dust
but all I find is empty bottles.
You will say they are mine.

Last night under a huge sky
I stepped outside and peered upwards .
You floated silently past,
in the white and silent shape of an owl,
eyes glittering with moon dust,
seeing me, and not seeing me at all.

When it's Yours

Genevieve Ray

We want to empathise
We want to build bridges
In the widening skies
To catch all fallen children
All the forgotten adults
And calm all lasting sorrows

But pain that is not ours
Needs to be handled softly
Trigger warn if you must do
More conscious option
Is to read as openly
If it isn't what you have felt

My experience as a teacher
Though no PGCE
In my itch hands
Has been that those
In the horrifying expanse
Talk in underlines

They have lived and breathed
The pain we don't want to imagine
They do not go to melodrama
Make Edgar Allen Poe horrors
They are so blindingly frank
And that is the bit that is painful

The eyes of a child mistreated
Are not glass balls of ice
They are hardened
And un-edited by Photoshop
They say so much in one word
And ultimately that breaks you

A forgotten person
Lives in forever transition

———

Having to bargain for attention
Choose dignity or mention
A burnish experience
Of having 'charity' fairly challenged

The poem I assessed
Struck me hard
A knowing of the truths
Buried under floorboards
If learning true empathy
Has been anything at all

The voice that knows
Always stings more
In frankness rather than prose
Killing the sermonising
And cutting at the throat

only days
Matt Elmore

what are these to be but only days?
to kiss to dream to slip away
for a moment in time, never to stay
what are these to be but only days?

what is life to be but only this?
to share to love to leave to miss
successful failure; oh wretched bliss!
what is life to be but only this?

what more to have but more to lose
to pay the toll with years as dues
the sun shall fall, then slowly fade
what are these to be but only days?

I try not to think about it

Matt Elmore

within a cliche cascade, I'm drowning
in sparkling dews of crude confounding
around paradise, troubles are surrounding
withstanding demands of dogs hounding
my drain is named, succumbing to shame
emptiness becomes my lack of accounting

fudged budget a wound, don't touch it
one nudge of a docket could flood it
a deep hole, even Everest could not plug it
of pleasured pyrite is this delightful nugget
tempestuous crest of measure I know best
has come up short on a budget of puppets

everyday foiled; to spring a theme uncoiled
broiled and boiled into tasteless burnt toil
sunshine on roses of dreams long spoiled
reveal seedless peels of promise now soiled
to slink as a fink on the brink of extinct
common within the soul of a mole once royal

I try not to think about it, thoughts rearranged
yet I've become estranged, my mind deranged
droughts of doubts without anything gained
turn to dust, entrusted to my informal remains
thus, I thrust my trust well into the dusk
for I must accept regrets I cannot change

I Never Did Learn

Lorna McLaren

I never did learn to read music
but played my tenor horn with pride,
I'd listen to how the piece sounded
and let that be my guide.

Crotchets, quavers, semibreves
were pictures on the score
though even with that lack of knowledge
I still played to the fore.

We'd march at Miners' Galas,
it made me feel so proud,
especially when I heard
the cheering of the crowd.

I no longer play,
those days are long gone now,
a memory from my teenage years
that just popped up somehow.

There were lots of fun times
while playing with the band
although at times when we were practising
we did get out of hand,
then we'd get a telling off
and get back to what we should.

I never did learn to read music
but I sometimes wish I could.

Oblated to Black

Emmelia M

they are talking about black,
in my never-ending nights,
obsolete to the colourless corpse,
once they have never been there,
since existence endures,
nights are foretold not to pretend.

they are flattering the insidious black,
even all pirates are standing with their clean hands,
uttermost seen are propaganda,
the black holds my nights densely,
my room is hooked with
his constant mortuary,
I confess in nothingness,
the evil stranded.

the black own his immortal missionary,
crews of testimonial voyage,
having no particular visages,
no entirety,
he holds my destined forlorn,
discreet admirations,
no discrepancies among long conversations,
I only grant him
the colours of my heart,
the heart he always seeks to,
the colours are his lighthouse.

candid smiles he saves implicitly,
for tomorrow we share and hold,
never promising any disclosed impurities,
the black in both are inseparable,
any gifted talents are miracles.

———

172

She
Tracey Louise Brunning

Her illusion swims in my mind,
Snaking up the tapered stem
of my wine glass,
dipping delicate toes
in the magenta liquid.
Sashaying round the rim,
hair trailing loose and wild,
curves melting into the vessel.
Laying wrapped like a coil
in the sediments that remain.

Life is a Dream
Archie Papa

Please do not wake me
for life is a dream
the pathways of fate
lead not where they seem

From the dancing of shadows
to music of light
from lush colored skies
to the still of the night

From the sweet smell of lilac
to trickles of rain
from pale sullen moonlight
in the crickets refrain

This life is a dream
from reason to rhyme
safe in my slumber
from the chaos of time

Dear Vincent

Donna Smith

Dear Vincent Van Gogh

My Apologies,
Your paintings are not what we are looking for,
They lack liveliness, freshness, and vigour.
Your lack of experience shows through in your strokes,
Starry night is offensively obscure.

It's all scribbles and swirls and your palette is bland,
It's old fashioned, the style is all wrong.
Strokes of an inexperienced, unstable young man,
It's rushed, hectic, manic, headlong.

The bedroom is plain, just yellow, and blue,
The house seems slightly askew.
You need to revisit, re-examine this piece,
Look again from a different aspect and view.

And why so many painting of sunflowers?
Why not a red rosebush in full bloom?
Spring crocuses in a field or a meadow,
That smell like sweet honey perfume.

What is your fascination with cafés?
Wine glasses adorned on tables and chairs.
It's seedy with a dark underbelly,
No panache, finesse, lacking in flair.

Your paintings aren't selling, your attitudes wrong,
You're abrasive, unsociable, and rude.
Your drunken episodes don't bode with the buyers,
In your psychotic, depressed, melancholy mood.

Your paintings are worthless, just throw them away,
You'll never get rich from your art.
You'll always be poor if you stay on this path,
Change your vocation and make a fresh start.

Dear Mrs Anna Carbentus van Gogh

Please accept my condolences, on the loss of your son,
His death is a loss to us all.
We'd love to make an offer on all of his art,
Enclosed you'll find the first install.

Your son was a genius, with exceptional skill,
We misjudged him, we misunderstood.
His work is outstanding, one of the best,
Extraordinary, exceptionally good.

Starry night is a masterpiece, one of a kind,
A magnificent depiction of the sky.
A light in the windows to guide people home,
A powerful message which made us all cry.

The bedroom shows balance and unity,
The crookedness in the room is unique.
The combination of colour is daring and bold,
He had a one-off distinctive technique.

The sunflower paintings are a triumph,
They resonate to the rich and the poor.
The colours are daring and striking,
Like nothing we've seen done before.

The Night Café is one of my favourites,
Giving the night life a completely fresh look.
It's expressive with an emotive use of colour,
Just like a picture from inside of a book.

We'd like to buy his entire collection,
Money's no object at all.
Adorn the museums with his beautiful art,
Maybe one or two for my living room wall.

Let's give him the recognition that he deserves,
It shouldn't have taken this long.
Tis a shame it's taken until after his death,
To shout his praise, before his final swan song.

Endless Pit
Esperanza Phillip

No lights shining
goosebumps all over
echoes screeching
not even a bounty of faith
can end the endless stones
raining in their reign
no swerves no summersaults
will end this facade
oh tears have flooded the ground
drowning a crystal of hope
heads spin deep within
life has become mean
like a raging thunder it has become
people expect it to be calm
people expect this to be over
they think lights will hover
and kiss them
in their savaged groans

The Cloud On Your Door
Rafik Romdhani

I have seen the cloud on your door disappear
and Infinity's dawn little by little draw near.
I have seen grass around your grave
implore God for more Summer rain.
I have seen those corn cobs writhe on fire,
slightly burning your fingers but you smile.
I have seen the breeze steer its direction
toward the furnace ready for your leaven.
I have seen you in a recent dream,
ploughing my laden heart with your eyes.

I have seen you raise your hands to the ceiling,
preventing its falling on my long ways.
I have seen pain's pearls run down your face
and very soon turn into sparkling stars.
I have seen the hammers of time
chasing you, completely break and dissolve.
I have seen you in the corridors of the mind.
But I feel like lost for words and almost dumb.
I have seen the cloud on your door disappear
and infinity's dawn little by little draw near.
I have seen you taking me to the great beyond.

The Siren Song
Karin J. Hobson

Irish mist kissed her lashes long
Cool breeze thru lone Hawthorn
Barefoot she danced with song
Sung ethereally to she.

Springs, Wells, Groves conform
Tales rail truthful norms
Did you see what used to be
The knight's castle?

In a boat afloat-haze drifting along
Fog horn blows-solo bows out
'Where are you beloved?' is
Her mindful shout.

A rose pressed between two sheets
of tempered blue glass bequeathed;
Into the stars did he, into seas she bleeds
The Sirens' Song is reached.

Thunderous Tale

Imelda Zapata Garcia

Thunder filled the corners
of the pages
spilt upon with tempest
from the gales
gushing out the quill held
by the master
deafening the lies told
through the rails

Swirling truth spins well
within the telling
storming past deceit
to vivid pretence
painting graphic images
with verbiage
leaving naught to chance
an ill defence

Wrought, a warping wonder
of enlightenment
with a wicked whisper
of a tale
though to those who ponder
with excitement
it's just a simple story
with regale

Progress of a Snail
Michael Balner

Lift your eyes, too long they've been
fixed on dirt beneath your shoes.
See the sky, the clouds are brewing,
but the sun is hidden in them, too.

Look at birds, so careless, so free,
will you find yourself, will you fly?
Feel your heart, its steady beat,
listen, it will never tell a lie.

Explore your mind, what if you find
more yourselves than you're ready to see?
Befriend them all, there's no point to fight,
they are you, and they will always be.

Make inner peace, acknowledge your needs,
your fears and rage, sorrows, regrets.
And now brace for progress of a snail,
it might take years longer than you expect.

Drink the Night Away
Lora Lee

I yearn to taste the moon's silvered glow,
To dance among flowers, the fragrance they bestow.
To don the earth's cloak, become one with its grace,
In nature's embrace, I'll find solace and space.
Let me quench my thirst with the moon's sweet wine,
Bathe my weary spirit in petals divine.
To sleep upon streams, their lullaby serene,
In the arms of water, find peace unforeseen.
And oh, to taste the stars, those celestial gems,
Unlocking secrets, like precious hymns,
Their essence upon my lips, a cosmic treat,
Transcending boundaries, making life complete.

Quantum
Gavin Prinsloo

A tiny orb glows with the power of suns, dormant,
as its destiny awaits,
Held within is realities core,
locked behind its quantum gates

Linked to another, each orb bound in a matrix
to serve its cause,
Creating the illusion of solidity,
vibrating without pause

Look deep into the realm of Creation's birth,
for nothing here ever dies,
For matter has no meaning,
for prying living eyes

Go closer to the glowing gate,
and release Pandora's dreams,
For each orb is another reality,
bursting at its seams

Now look outward to the vaulted night,
and see the flotsam rotating around its core,
For when you peer inward you will see outward too,
when you gaze through Creation's door

Universe upon universe connected,
each within a glowing orb of light,
Existing as part of matter's creation,
stretching out into eternity's night

For quantum does not lay deep within,
for all occupies matter and space,
Reality is far removed from imagination,
as we gaze upon Creation's face

A Good Day
Terry Bridges

I scrape the sheer indelible blue of the sky
To colour my days when rain descends
I know the ways of sunshine's flattery
The weather is always what we apprehend
I surrender to the isobar's majesty
Googling every hour for the latest trends
Nothing new in our fixation on tragedy
Like always thinking the worst of our friends
But this magnificent evening like an ecstasy
Glows in my fiery heart and transcends

The Morning Song
Dale Parsons

The sun is yet to rise but the bird it sings,
Open tired eyes and curse the monster's wings.
Just one more hour of sleep, please allow me that,
Damn your morning song, you little feathered prat.
Who do you think you are, waking up the street?
No one wants your chirps, your whistles or your tweets.
Just one more hour of sleep, remain quiet in your nest,
Shut that beak of yours, please let this fellow rest.
The sun is yet to shine, yet you chatter still,
Horrid little creature with a horrid little shrill.
To wake a man so early can really make him bitter,
To wake a man so early with that awful morning twitter.
This man just wants to sleep, roll over in his covers,
Now that's not going to be, you've awoken countless others.
One hundred nasty birds now join your singalong,
One hundred nasty birds, damn your morning song.
The rustle in the leaves and the racket from the trees,
Leaves a man no option... Get up a make some tea.

Lost
Graeme Stokes

Did I lose life or did life lose me?
It's now so dark,
that it's too hard to see
So far in the wilderness, stranded at sea
Did I lose life or did life lose me?

The Ladder of Life
Paul G Holroyd

I'm past the halfway mark as I climb towards the dark never
knowing when my journey's going to end
Glancing down the rungs I've passed feels like I climbed it way too
fast but the only choice I have now is ascend

It only makes me sadder that I can't descend the ladder unless I lose
my grip and plummet down
Seeing all my life flash by in the blinking of an eye before my steps
all crumble back into the ground

On my climb I often find lots more ladders intertwined, some stay
with me and others drift apart
Occasionally they fall or they never climb at all, a broken ladder
means a broken heart

So I cling for dear life through the laughter and the strife and keep
my footing firmly on the rungs
One step at a time as I make the steady climb as long as there's still
air inside my lungs

My ending might be soon or I could climb to the moon, nobody
knows the moment they will fall
Unless they hit a slump and decide they'd rather jump, I hope that
feeling never comes to call

Love is a Scared Curlew
Rafik Romdhani

I looked in all the books
for the way that leads to you
The glass of wine dancing
in my hand breaks in two.
I looked for the key to everything
that may keep fire glowing.
Love is a scared curlew
with worn out feet like reeds
in deep quicksand drowning.
I looked in all the books
for what may bring you back
and draw your face closer.
The flung distance between us
is certainly a mistake
where the tempest has laid
the toughest stones
and swiftly passed.
I searched among all of them
for our lost footprints.
I read all the open windows
but none echoed your depths.

Steps of Olympus
Gregory Richard Barden

I filled my heart with music of the moon
thus pulled it close about me like a wrap
my tympans gently trembled with a tune
I held my breath of starlight
and danced upon the dune
a-scratching in the sand, a manic map

I plunged into a pool of passions, pure
to swim the depths in vigor and delight
each wake of wonder, sensual and sure

183

a dream to deftly drown in
of damsel craves, demure
amid the dark abyssal brine of night

I bargained with a god upon the peaks
to walk abreast the clouds, as if the sea
and plumb for souls as deity so seeks
yet all the nets pulled empty
come barren, silence speaks
not due an effort, worship or decree

I stained a cloak of love with dim neglect
but painted my remorse upon the skies
so each new blushing morn would so reflect
how beautiful the earth was
through nature's grand affect
to grace even the least beholden eyes …

and leave each heart, as mine …
to heaven's guise.

Fragments of My Being

Aaron Blackie

I will break my being as fragments
Of deluge,
And makes it count in the library,
Where destiny longs for the fingers
Of purpose...

I will slice in pieces,
Foliage of my heart into
Miniature arteries,
And cause them to form into
Diversities of bloodlines
Spreading, coagulating, clothing
Into branches of leaves, budding
Fruitage of compassion...

I will pour out my essence,
Like waterfall, from
The heated cup of adversity,
And makes it flow
Into steadied rivers of memories —
Confluent network of wholly healings...

I will bend my waist and stretched
My backbone...
If only to craft meanings out
of those human delusions,
Spinning in bubbles and in circles...

Stretch me then, O, stretch me,
Soul-curious antennae...
Hooked to the human nature
And be me,
Metamorphosis into sweet
Nectareous flowers
Of eternal scars for healing balms,
And ashes for firmaments
Of beauty and grace...

The Moon in My Hand
Donna Smith

I clasp the moon in my hands,
It illuminates all that hides in the shadow.
Casting light upon all within my vision,
A wondrous gift it does bestow.

I hold the shine of the sun in my eyes,
Its sprinkled iridescent stardust abounds.
It lights my footsteps wherever I tread,
Son et Lumiere forms on the ground.

I reach for the shimmering stars,
Through the inky black they show me their light.
Their lustre gleams guiding me onwards,
Providing a small glint, a chink into the night.

I grasp for the cumulus clouds,
As they form white cotton balls in the sky.
They cushion and cosset as I journey forward,
Reforming and changing as I pass on by.

I embrace the world underneath my feet,
It leads me down new paths and road.
Guides me in the right direction,
Dust off my shackles, release my heavy load.

After the Rain
Lorna McLaren

Yesterday it rained non-stop,
reflections of my mood,
raindrops snaked down my window
obstructing what I viewed,
like in the way you see the world
as tears spring from your eyes
almost as if the world you observe
has put on a disguise.
Today the day dawned bright and clear,
hardly a cloud in sight,
a perfect day for walking
and so I thought I might.
Avoiding all the puddles
that were left behind,
I felt the sea air fill my lungs
and also clear my mind.
Yet in the wake of all the rain
Nature never ceases to amaze
reflections of the sky and clouds
is on what I now gaze.
An island in a giant puddle,
growing there a clump of trees,
but isn't it so wonderful
when she gives us sights like these.

Fall
Chadwick Lewis

If this be the end, let fall be my time,
let none there weep, nor pay me no mind.

Let not ravens land soft on my grave,
nor offer any prayers for the gifts never gave.

Salt my bones so never can return,
the ghost of your memory or the kiss of your burn.

Scatter my words like crumbs in a tale
so each there in my yearn if for a spell.

To taste the seasons of days long passed,
no stones in the brook of firsts and their lasts....

Rising Above
Gavin Prinsloo

What hands are dealt in fickle whim,
when hope seeks to rise above,
When confusion reigns when you seek the truth,
looking down from love?

Clouds seeded with hopes and dreams,
the flotsam of a myriad thought,
Floating above the clouds of dreams,
where love has come to naught

Place your tread upon the billowing path,
let imagination roll the dice,
Let the cards fall where reason ends,
where love pays insanity's price

Cumulus Consecration

Hahona Pita Batt

Cumulus buckles under the weight of the sun
silken skies bequeath Aphrodite's eye
filagree shapes frolic in marshmallow dance
clouds slowly part like detangled lovers
threadbare sky apparitions
dragon tale plumes meld with oblivion
jaundiced winds exhale
gentle breeze spent giants
whistling melodies
supernal heavenly notes
Cupid arrow artisans' strums
Mandolin succulent tones
ears pricked in sensuous gloat
cumulae marionettes join us in conjugal foray
cloud cosseted divinity in celestial play
winds of revelation fill our sails
whimsical lovers enthralled
destiny etched in hieroglyph
hearts tithed to eternal sky
cumulus consecrated sacred vowels
sentient love sworn betrothal
our nimbus coverture embrace.

When Winter Takes a Final Bow

Trude Foster

When winter takes a final bow
he does not sever all his ties with spring
nor summer when she passes on her crown
each takes the best of what the others bring

Let Me Love You...Forever
Hisham Hawwa

passed...past...years
broken the cup of cheers
grown up the trees of tears...
altered home...honeycombed
home was once a dome,
but birds migrated their nests,
mirth masticated to mess,
dearth defenselessly dressed;
now, in a droughted desert,
hearth's fest was at its best
heart's crest is at its west
now, rests in the vest:
in dust and gust and rust

kismet makes fool of us
life plays games with us
time taunts us,
so, let me love you...forever
threefold more...together

moonlight mercurially mirrors
monsoon murky murders —
love that once melted our lips
and raptured our ribs...
recaptured our scarred eyes
and stitched our salted skies...
now, you can't see me...anymore
the night is long...very long
lopped is the lung...split is the song...
hearth's fest was at its best
heart's crest is at its west
now, rests in the vest:
in dust and gust and rust

were we to fold brine in cans
were we to hold time in hands
and defy fate...with open gates

if and only if…
were we to make heaven merry…
were we to wake sweven saintly…
and step over the threshold…
before limbs get cold…
if and only if…

sea waves moan…worn winds
a sailor and oar…grown grinned
groaned, thinned thick with frost…lost…
our date was in the cradle of dreams
our plate was on table of the teens
yet, nights narcotized to nibble routine
sunshine sterilized to sable steams
wordless warm words
are spoken in silence
sighs seemed to whirl
screaming in sequence…

my cup and wine,
my shine and shrine,
My Desideratum!
my sup and rhyme
my mine and spine,
My Sanctum
to you, I speak my silence
for you, I seek my essence
you are my voice…my rejoice
you are my birth and breath…
my depth and my wealth

kismet makes fool of us
life plays games with us
time taunts us,
so let me love you…forever
threefold more…
to the hardest of core…together

regret recedes down my memory
for things that will never be, never be

for the seeds of our passion
are days and desire and devotion
cafés and fire and fixation
God, how to return youth
and soul to soothe?!

to you I speak my silence
for you I seek my essence
you are my voice…my rejoice
you are my birth and my breath
my depth and my wealth

Proximity to Homelessness
Joseph Andrew Miller

This odd little crayon
Lives in the corner
Of a miscellaneous drawer

There isn't the space
In the big carton for it
In a set missing some colors

Its wax is not waxy
Too bright or too dim
Not enough like all the others

Nicked up and worn
Wrap faded and torn
Better than lost to the floor

I Am

Claire Victoria Sutton Williams

I am the autumn leaves that fall
I am the trees that stand so tall
I am the stars twinkling at night
I am the sunshine, I am the light
I am the winter chill that blows
I am the beautiful summer rose
I am the sweet fragrant scent
I am the dreams that came and went
I am the clouds up above
I am the thing
That you call love
I am the one that you feel near
Never forget me
I am always here.

Glass of Hours

Imelda Zapata Garcia

I hear the ticking of the moments
wasting as breath escapes my brow
whispers of mist, collect the hours
binding them to some broken bough

growing, glowing in the dimming light
as dusk crawls near, a clamoring sound
wraps the space which draws to close
the fleeting glances that abound

written, in the sands which pour
swiftly through the space allowed
oaths which often go unspoken
gone like other pledges vowed

Tremors
Adiela Michael Osiah

Underneath my feet
These thoughts fly,
I'm weak beneath
My fears bar me
I could spell them out
But they elude me.

Above my smiles
They lurk as darkness,
My soul tries to be free
But freedom is but a shadow
A shadow I never could get.

Undecided are my words
They are but lingering echoes,
They fill me with questions
Questions I seek
These are my pleas
They're always on deaf ears.

Save me from these tremors
They don't see my pleas,
I am but asking
Asking to be noticed
This echo is hoping to be heard
Save me lest I'm tossed away.

I'm ready to learn
Learn the ways of peace,
Teach me so I can know
These troubled waters are here
Here to drown me once again
Help me beyond my dreams
Before these fangs sink into me
I await your voice…

When Just a Boy
Michael W. Hamel

When just a boy you held me tight,
Through pain, and tears, and fright
I felt your fingers through my hair,
To show me it's alright

Then as I grew I questioned things,
It seemed like all the time
I'd worry of the fears it brings,
You'd sing a little rhyme

I became a man and then moved out,
To grow through when and where
When times were hard I'd think about,
How you are always there

This would bring a soothing calm,
Your words of love and care
Like a soothing, scented balm,
And you were always there.

What's on Your Mind?
Kenneth Wheeler

The mind is an ocean of passion and pride
A place where emotions can suffer or hide,
It's a window of pleasure of memories unseen,
that appears in our visions, flooding our dreams,
It's a periscope of things that we longs to forget,
Of moments of failure or endless regrets,
They will appear in our dreams with devastating effects —
You long for them to sink into the deepest sea,
but you know they will resurface, in another dream.
The mind is an ocean of stormy emotions,
That can melt the hardest, meanest heart,
It can cause such pain and discomfort

Within, a fearful grief stricken heart,
One longs for it to stop, to go away, to depart,
Because the distress is tearing at one's heart,
Like falling to earth, with no one to help
Or drowning in a vile sea, where regret is felt
It's a whirlwind of sadness of love we have lost
No longer present with us here in real life,
but they well often appear in our dreams
filling us with joy and endless delight
But suddenly they depart we are left alone,
Our tender emotions are growing cold.
Yes, the mind can be so active bringing
Joy or misery, it depends on the mood
We were in when we climb into our beds,
that will decide our programme tonight.
Our minds can be active in many ways,
giving us hours of magical display,
Or fills our night with fear and stress.
Or the face of love ones, we feel blessed.
But I must admit our love a bit of a trip,
Down that road of my mind, the program
Is always different, so if you don't mind.
I'm going to sleep, to see what's on
The program in my mind — showing tonight.

The Trinity Test
Iain Strachan

To break the very atoms forced apart
Not God, but man was bending nature's claws
A fission chain-reaction at its heart.
Refiner's fire he thought would end all wars.
The tree of knowledge bore its tainting fruit:
Plutonium — a sphere of grapefruit size
And neutrons, spreading virus-like to boot
The kilotons to hell, a monstrous prize.
As he beheld the fiery blooming cloud
A revelation filled the screaming flames

The Hindu scripture spoke as if aloud
Confronted him, pronounced these fearful names —
A World-Destroyer, now becoming Death,
And guilt to haunt him till his final breath.

Anaemic Skies

Graeme Stokes

Their days don't have the rays,
they lack the sustenance that's required
In rains in stratospheric aches,
too much to keep their powder dry
Neck deep in austerity, acumen walks tranquilised
Their clumsy gropes for levity,
are mocked and marginalised
For its juvenile delinquency,
the sun can only apologise
But they're picking up the frequency,
breaking through anaemic skies

The silence speaks in volumes, their hope bleeds brutalised
Ambition chokes in acrid plumes, dust settles reconciled
Expectation fires desires, a redundant exercise
To question why it conspires,
leaves them broke and stigmatised
But grey gives way to cautious blue, an art of compromise
If only for the fleeting few, some fare for anaemic skies

Hysterical tears of apathy, they can't recognise the signs
Cold brick walls of empathy, doors long since pulverised
The belief will surely kill them, yet mistrust will jeopardise
Circumstance already grills them, vitality in short supply
Their pallid face will glow once more,
hunger starts to moisturise
Optimism starts to forge,
sun bursts through anaemic skies

Days Night
Sarah Wheatley Tillbrook

As sun of day, day turns to moon of night
He says, it's your turn to light the skies
Fill the world with lullabies
And with sweet surrendered sighs
All if right, all is fine
As soft beds release the minds
And their consciousness combine
With the images behind
It was illusive for dark time
Now the meaning is imbibed
And they bid the past goodbye
With the understanding why
As the sun of day turns from moon of night
And they see that all's all right

Silhouette
Imelda Zapata Garcia

the shades are drawn and yet
your figure does appear to dance
the sheen of moonlit stardust lifts
to press upon a darkened sliver
a most pronounced, appearance
of character in supple evidence
a silhouette of your embrace
that to this day does bring a shiver

lustrous color sets the brilliance
illuminating lasting backdrop
this August moon leaves me aghast
with promise of unconditional returns
though truth be told, reality foretold
no such thing would sooner crop
since in the ether where you dwell
the candle of your breath

no longer burns

why then, this pledge of sorrow
a shadow of those brighter moons
how does your form emerge this
ill begotten loom, to torment
ages have slipped from reach
long gone, those forgotten tunes
drawn out hours lost moments
are the only memory spent

a likeness, etched by the shining
leaves your loved ones pining
there is no regret in struggling to forget
what yesterday stole upon demise
oh tolerant orb, take your sign
no need to reflect on silver lining
a soul that's farthest from restore
there cannot be an ever more reprise

It Mattered Not
Eugene Winslow

It mattered not the hows and whens,
the reasons why, the nows and thens,
This life is none but parody
of whatever's willed to be
There is so much to do and see
in redefined reality

To write a poem and have a thought,
To express oneself to astro-naught,
the spirit of a God of life,
the paradox of our existence

Trinity
Steve Wheeler

Inside the manmade mist Thor's fist
resounds like comets ride, collide
with hammered orb. Obituary
marking a planetary suicide.

Then Aether's lethal chorus rides
upon the drums of dark delight
and blinks his jaded gimlet eye
toward a cold celestial light.

The limbs of thought devise out-wise,
ensnared in candid fleeting space,
conducting tragic symphonies
behind enigma's black embrace.

There Odin's tapestry be-weaves
a fractal wave, wild and obscene
across a blackened verge, converged
time's molten secret force unseen.

In shadowed veils the arcane fifth
dimension burns obscure. Unseen
by skeins of toxic paradox,
dichotic truth and lies convene.

Lessons from Shadows

Caroline Rodgers

From the darkness of abuse's cruel reign,
Lessons emerged, resilience gained.
To speak my mind, to stand up tall,
Breaking free from the oppressor's thrall.

In defiance of control, I found my voice,
No longer trapped, I made my choice.
To wear my truth, my colors bold,
Embracing imperfections, a story untold.

Lessons learned from pain endured,
A spirit awakened, once obscured.
I rise against chains that sought to bind,
Discovering strength, a liberated mind.

Shattered Rain

Gavin Prinsloo

Storms rage against a mind rebuffed,
weathered beyond repair or grief,
Isolated in showers of regret and hope,
desperately assuming faiths belief

Walking alone through alleys blind,
the next corner bleeds the deepest dark,
No force of nature can illume the heart,
weathered now cold and stark

Head bent down against the raging winds,
hail and sleet beat against a crown of pain,
An umbrella of hope fades away into the dark of night,
battered and cracked by shattered rain

Daydream Stupor
Hahona Pita Batt

From beneath welled eyes
I build castles in the sky
Eyelid moats stem a weeping tide
Tears loft in skyscraper accretion plume
Eyelash oars avail oasis shores

Epoch epistle in simile faceted smile
Dreams anchored in burlesque oceans
Saline precipitate in chimera rhapsody
Salt encrusted tight rope brow
Inclement storms engorge this portend

Minnow mind cossets driftwood detritus
Flotsam and jettisoned thoughts
ruminate in lifeboat squall
Rosary sweat beads fall like emancipated concubines
Briny tongue cuts swathes in optic time

Life rendered Philistine
in jocular plethora
I was to be — or wasn't I to be?
Evanescent ancestry in gild-less loin
Syntax camouflaged propaganda
Therein lies my flummoxed paradox

Crest fallen upon equinoxial leaf litter
Photosynthesis of a troglodyte son
Pacifist yield in perpetual surrender
Plying castles 'neath an easel sky
Orphic benefactor in crystal diadem
Cerebellum residue
in onamastic dialect construct
Daydream stupor in
philharmonic word
woven stanza
A protagonists
philosophical bonanza!

Absent Without Life

Neil Forsyth

Good morning,
Says the fantasist,
With hope set in his eyes,
He dreams away reality,
Of his non-existent life.

For existing is his by-word,
In his daily living hell,
Protected in his safe zone,
Hiding in his shell.

His day is long and weary,
His bed 'a happy place'
Shielded in his lonely world,
The one he cannot face.

This private hell it lingers,
It has done for a while,
Does happiness exist?

Within his distant smile.
He craves a healthy past,
When he felt no silent pain,
Then wonders if his good times,
Will ever come again!

Sun Rise, Sun Sets

Farha Abbasi

Maybe I am not there as a whole
And only exist in pieces now
The befores and afters
somewhere in between
Sun rise sun sets
Day begins night ends
Love like tides
Uproars and subsides
Not on the shore
in mayhem of the waves
Not in the noise of seagulls
in the silence of the shells
Not in laughter or tears
Not in hopes or fears
Maybe in a prayer
Not serene nor tranquil
At peace or in turmoil
Not real not virtual
A thought a sigh a wish in your heart
Don't seek me in light
Feel me in the dark
May be I exist only in realms of imagination
Or in a garden of adulations
Wilting and growing again
Maybe I am in grains of sand
slipping through your fingers
The more you try to hold
The more I slip away
Maybe one day I will be whole again
All the pieces melded
Cracks filled with gold
Stand up proudly
As no more broken vase

Water

Jon Wright

Memories running through my fingers
Thoughts in my mind lingers
Before they drift away like dust
False memories I no longer trust
My families faces drift like feathers on a breeze
Falling like leaves from the trees
My future shrouded in mist
My past memories no longer exist

My thoughts burn like wood in the fire
The book of songs empty for the choir
Songs are nothing but silence so deafening
As I stumble towards my final reckoning
My family my friends, like water in my hand
My memories grains of sand
Running through my fingers so fast
Disappearing till the very last

Until the last grain
The last drop of rain
The last memory fades like a ghost
But what hurts the most
Is losing you twice
Everything melting like ice
The only water left are tears that fall to the floor
Flooding my world as you close your final door
The sun rises in the early dawn
As memories drift away, as you are gone…

A Posthumous Poem
Hisham Ismail Hawwa

...there dwells a pitfall in every poem
it spells mayhem, nightfall in tandem,
...maybe a totem...of unsung stranger,
a token, hung dead...in a funeral procession...
breathless is the lung-natural to hell or heaven...
pulseless parading, followed by others in concession,
with bowed head, he paid obeisance,
to a narrow murky meadow...
in respect, corny complaisance...
abject acceptance...affirmation...
...
"deaths delivers many aches
and the achiest of which
is that of life"
...
see or seen...saline or serene
decreed or guaranteed,
scene of absurd world
not heard like a bird carrying words
not to unfurl his sateen pall,
he kept in a wall-less wall
inside the door of host-less hall...
inside the floor of tintless thrall...
of not to tell the truth!
what Truth?! I wonder...
...
like us, he strived and survived
and was deprived and...died,
for he didn't need to try that evening
for he didn't weep that morning
for he didn't cry in mourning
for he didn't sigh in sorrowing
for he didn't sign sufferings shadowing
people alive are brethren to the dead
the dead are legends with lost thread
wedded to dread or tread or be trodden

broken...forgotten...skeleton unspoken...
seem as if in seamless sleep...
all leak to the same reckless reek...
...

he was just a mundane man...a machine...
he did what he sustains, what can...routine...
he ended as he again began
and all human beings
are of the same clay:
war with living day by day
all go through the same gateway
at a point, they decay
...they expire...
they attire in dire
...respire in mire...
kick the bucket
...straitjacket...shut socket...
life busted, disgusted
...dusted...rusted...
like running out, they retire
to the wester-most wire
...and the forgone fire...
in cloudburst, proceed to the same place
they share the shroud, same space
...
...and here spawns the perfect poem
...tone in the rain
an emblem diadem dawns in bones
...again
...and again

Autumn's Palette

Fouzia Sheikh

Autumn's palette steals
the season's show
its hues of oranges
yellows and red aglow
Scarlet maples
burn down the season
over the mountain, hill, wood
and vale
against which other seasons'
colours pale
Blue spruces hug
the mountains like fog
The Autumn fog appears
as if the sleepy town smokes
Rain recalls the memory
Autumn paints with
a full palette

Invisible Poets

J Henry DeKnight

Too many invisible poets
waiting to be seen
Climbing branches
of the trees
with faded colour green
Too many hearts
left unbeating
too many souls in the fire
Invisible poets get lonely
for passion and love
and desire...

Die Not to the Anger of that Night

Hussaini Bukar

Oh! I have seen the real in you
That fireflies, yet fly to ride
In stagnant kite, the flowing winds
In climbed midst, the angering sky
Growing tall of jealous seed
To jerk night, feed not the soul to vain

To glamouring light, the flirting rise
In usher leaf, the crying noon
Null youth of embellish life
To cripple ride, never a dead ash

Oh! Die not to the sorrows winds
For winds, never a wish
To blink pink, not a rhyme
In blank, blank of versing stoop

Oh! Never a call, never a thought
Die not to the sorrow of that night
To night, is night

In felt breathe of pricing smile
Breath not the anger in youth
To colour, is unique spade

In town yard, the caring root
Die not, die not, to angering youth
To angering feet, is aging devil
In drummed midst, liberate flank

In silly grow of watering sky
Oh! Die not, die not to that night in anger
To fresh soul is icy treasure

Into the Dark
Terry Bridges

This thin bare tapestry of dusk
Fading light scatters across the grass
Ask nothing of immeasurable night
At the winding down of daily tasks
The owl of Minerva hoots a welcome
To the sleepless creations of restless minds
Horror fascination excitement all comes to this
One person's nightmare is another's bliss
Separate distinct moments share similar fates
Evaporate like dew-drops in watery moonlight
The black fractured silent hours await

Serpent Tongue
Steve Wheeler

There is no serpent like the angry tongue
Dark in the dangers of its tortured spite
Out from whose core a poisoned bile is wrung
Hell hath no venom like the Hydra's bite

Dark in the dangers of its tortured spite
Conjured in chambers full of falsehoods flung
Hell hath no venom like the hydra's bite
It sucks the marrow from a chorus sung

Conjured in chambers full of falsehoods flung
Its teeth will gnaw the soul of brutal night
It sucks the marrow from a chorus sung
And bleeds it slowly in the dawn's stale light

Its teeth will gnaw the soul of brutal night
Out from whose core a poisoned bile is wrung
And bleeds it slowly in the dawn's stale light
There is no serpent like the angry tongue

Dysthymia

Amanda Wilson

Over fatigue, intense daily burnout,
mental exhaustion, they physically weep.
Secondary trauma they're left in no doubt,
absence of value inherently deep.
Intrusive thoughts they'll paradoxically sleep.
Overwhelming anxiety, again relapse,
sinking into depression, nervous collapse.

Feeling disinterest, life of dispassion,
motivation left wanting, upheaval time.
Smile through distress with facial expression,
mental mountain with depression to climb.
Abyss descending will this last a lifetime?
Considered a nobody, failure to shine,
inability to flourish, that life, mine.

My soul departed, emotions reject,
feelings discouraged, no aspiration.
Internal scream, undesirable effect,
brain on overload, disinclination.
Heightened awareness of the depression.
Dysthymia weighs heavy, body and soul,
a heart now broken as it's torn its hole.

A shelled former self, lost in the shadow,
faith In destiny, a lifetime I'd hoped.
Shadowlands dark, apparent and shallow,
devastative inability to cope.
Just a part of life, this slippery slope?
Lacked sense of meaningless profound this day,
but forevermore life won't remain this way.

Support is essential, reach out it's your life,
positive energy inner health, well-being.
Disconnection freedom from numbness, strife,
physical, emotional, welfare, start feeling.
Process entrust, empowerment, new being.
Mindset needs adjustment, from depressive malaise,
unlimited potential, forthcoming appraise.

I Park My Mind
Jan Kenneth Velle

i park my mind
in your tolerated sky
i pound on my grace
hitting the wall
as our insecure falls
i tremble on your cause
falling into your arms
in the point of no return
while the dagger sink
and hours to think
limps across a silent mountain
descending every star
in the blossom of a heart
where i collide in between
holding on to the substance
of every hiding
in all collapse
i wear my crown

If only I had Left a Trace
Sali Andiamo Wamastarpack

If only I had left a trace
Now that I'm nowhere to be found
With no one along to embrace
I keep going round and round

Now that I'm nowhere to be found
I covered up my footprints so they can't track
I keep on going round and round
With the cracking of the ground I can't go back

I covered up my footprints so they can't track
It's so cold and dark still I am all alone
With the cracking of the ground I can't go back

I'm inside a stone my whereabouts are unknown

It's so cold and dark still I am all alone
To say that I'm in heaven but now it's all hell
I'm inside a stone my whereabouts are unknown
Rang me a bell tell them to wish me well

To say that I'm in heaven but now it's all hell
With no one along to embrace
Rang me a bell tell them to wish me well
If only I had left a trace

Succumb or Surmount
Farha Abbasi

Succumb or surmount
Tumultuous waves
Life twists and turns
Washes over
Drenching challenging questioning
Stand up fall down
Unstable in the moving sands
Skin scorched eyes burns adverse events
Like burning sun rising tides
Failing strides give up
Or get up one more time
Drown in sorrows
Even in pain smile
Falter fail ride the wave succumb
Or surmount
Never a choice
Face the setting sun
With faith and knowledge rise again
armor of resilience
And of unwavering courage
Wear the badge of bravery
not as a survivor
But the proud warrior
You are ...

Spiritual Skulduggery

Eric Aguilar

By the hot coals of the potter's oven,
the soul is refined; distilled of all ill will.
The Ghost of Holy waft grows seeds.

At the call of just a whisper,
and two ears of a silenced tongue,
the heart listens to the wailing wind.

Receiving deceit by devices.

The truce is a varied pitch of tone
in style, technique and harmony.
Lifting evils' veils sights the blind.

In the throes of a great cloak
lie Spiritual skulduggery.

A Puzzle

Bernard Pearson

She used to switch on the sun
Making it shine especially for us.
Now the chalice of P.G. Tips
Her spindle finger caress
Too weak to bring to lips.
Once a crossword fiend,
Now every clue begins,
A blank.
She sits upon her
Fire proof throne,
In the communal area
Yet all alone.
She waits for God or Godot,
While round about her
Aproned ladies fuss,

and feed their flock
as she had once done.
I leave her looking
Straight ahead
And make it
To the door
Before I cry.
Thankfully,
She's far too
busy waiting,
to hear my
whispered,
superfluous,
long,
goodbye.

You Hear
Karin J. Hobson

You hear the ethers whispers
Coming of wisdom's woes
Flooded archways collared reaches
Rust of silver and of gold
Empty hands, but full pockets
Power of punishment unfolds
One day one thousand years
One thousand years a day
Repentance of soaked cloth
Warmth on winter days, alas!

Patience like a smouldering fire
Yet, intense heat cometh
Without water bucket sold
Destruction in way of tenfold

Sleepwalk speaks of inner deep
Dragonflies like angels lie

Word of mouth are deep waters
Fountain's wisdom flows like brook

Sun shines atop glass table
Tempered no doubt by past
Book of Enoch misspoke of Abel
She knows not this fable

Slain are tossed like withered leaf
No belief no relief
He who strokes the quill
Now offers no more thrills

When I Fall

Ian Hall

When I fall
Dance with me
With the leaves and wind
In the moonlit forest

Take me down
A no name stream
Onto an ancient river

Suffocate me
And crush my chest
Underneath
The collapsing glass of
Ocean waves

Wash me up
All broken up
on an a golden beach
To dance once more
With the sand and wind

Eclipsing

Caroline Rodgers

Once trapped within a haunted mind,
Demons danced, a torment unkind,
Flashbacks sliced through like shards of glass,
Nightmares held in an iron grasp.

Avoidance ruled, a refuge sought,
Hyperarousal's battles fought,
A storm of feelings, thoughts so bleak,
A spirit fragile, heart left weak.

Bed became a prison, heavy stone,
Demons whispered, you're all alone,
But from the depths, a spark did rise,
A glimmer of hope, a will to prize.

Gathering strength, a slow ascent,
Taming the demons that once were bent,
With courage forged from deep within,
The journey started to begin.

Holding the reins, control reclaimed,
Each step forward, the past untamed,
Over time, the storm grew still,
As resilience triumphed over ill.

Five years turned six, a tale unfold,
A spirit rising, brave and bold,
From shadows cast, to light so clear,
Taking back the life once held dear.

No longer chained, no longer confined,
Those demons subdued, now left behind,
A journey fought, a victory won,
From battles lost, a new life spun.

Hallowed Hall

Gav Oliver

Hallowed hall,
where strange dreams manifest and spirits call.

Crimson veil of slumbers fall.
Asleep, yet not, symbols and signs weave
in twilight shadows standing tall.

Dragons dance, Druids trance,
answer the riddle, take a chance.

Sparks of recognition
from ancestral memories shrouded.
In a tomorrow yet to be, there by the light of divinity
we can clear the mind clouded.

Soft whispers, wafer thin slivers, nocturnal shivers.
Reality breaks down as you claim the golden crown.

Turning of the page, open to the invocations
of your inner mage.
Remember, sacred is your soul, and receive.
Remember, wisdom and knowledge come
in mysterious ways never to deceive.

Dragons dance, Druids trance,
answer the riddle, take a chance.

Deep is the well of the soul, crystal are the waters within.
Dark is the forest of deception, twisted are its roots of
illusion.

Moonlight, starbright, silver and gold.
Remember the name of your magnificence,
oh so beautiful and so very, very old.

Asleep in the twilight, awakening in the morning light.
Reignited in the fires of spiritual insight.

Dragons dance, Druids trance,
answer the riddle, take a chance.

What's at Stake

Joseph Gallagher

Before Shakespeare invented the anti-hero
Before DaVinci discovered the dark side of the moon,
Before the star's eyelids were wrapped in silk
Because their beauty was too much to bear...
That's when the soul whispers for you to draw near
And sings if you were any more stunning
Surely I would be blinded, surely my spirit would break—
I answered, 'Let my heart be what's at stake.'

I never claimed darkness was my father
Or that the road I walked on was called despair.
I may be foolish for believing that the wind remembers
Our sorrows and carries them clean to the sea...
They rise, an aroma of roses to nimbus clouds of rain
The winds wish to wash us fresh of our reoccurring pain.
Our memories hold them down beneath a depthless lake—
I must remember to let my heart be what's at stake.

I saw a dancer in red high heels leap skyward
On a moon strewn beach in Old Orchard Maine.
She seemed to levitate just above the Boardwalk,
In that instant I imagined the concept of the soul
Caught between time and space, here and now,
Between body and blood and whatever comes next...
Like a dream of a place where the soul comes to sleep,
And if it dies before I wake—
Let my heart be what's at stake.

And if our silence or our prayers cut us loose,
Suspended in time, let us go falling from our doubts
Like highwire acrobats without a net...
Our arches curved, our spines like smoke
Ready if not eager to break from all we grieve,
Prepared like ghosts to disappear, to take our leave.
Our lives are what we think, do, feel and make—
Let our hearts be what's at stake.

In this Wasteland

Amanda Wilson

In the great outdoors, fix your gaze on the moors,
at the purple hue of the heather.
The sunshine it peeps, the moon it now sleeps
awaiting the change in the weather.

The billowing breeze, through the few sunlit trees,
the Willows they sway amongst gorse.
The spring has now sprung,
the curlews begun to sing on the wing with full force.

Those Curlews in Spring, the Lapwings on wing,
the Woodlark, the Warbler and Nightjar.
Those birds that nest low, where bracken does grow,
keeps them safely under the radar.

The Birch trees they sway, and so starts the day,
look far across the heathland.
The Blackberries bear fruit and Bilberries follow suit,
life still unearths a way in the wasteland.

The tree of life Rowan, grows on the common,
white flowers they turn into berries.
They need picking and pressing, preserving and dressing,
supplying all manner of jellies.

In this wild barren farmland, this infertile heathland,
or that is the way it would seem.
But with adders, worms and newts that all contributes,
to a rare ecological dream.

Celestial Opus
Hahona Pita Batt

An opus in the cosmos
a romantic renaissance
Artisans strum
the chords of Saturn
Venus rises
in unadulterated foreplay
an intoxicating potpourri

Overtures play
in the crucible of my heart
My *Mon Cheri*
My supernal moon enchantress
no need for rhyme
in synchronization
The gravity of this seduction
tantamount to abduction
of naive innocence

Yet so willingly
I oblige your invitation
Silent voices
of conscience relegated
That foreign ignoramus
pragmatism expelled
Your advances gladly reciprocated
within this sentient corporeal entity

A benefactors heart enraptured
Silvery shawls
and silky threads of gold
Celestial body bewitchery
woven heartstring entrancement
a sublime entanglement

Resplendent in
ethereal sumptuousness
a liaison preordained

and extolled by the gods
I am as Adam
awash in the flavor of you
A veritable garden of Eden

Bone of my bone
flesh of my flesh
I yield in a rapturous
rhapsody of essence
A sanctified union
as if foretold
in the crucible of creation
A lovers cathartic
consummation
of creation

Cosmicality
Lorna McLaren

Floating on a dream,
carried on a feather,
with a fragile silken thread
being my only tether.
Such a surreal feeling
in the infinity of space
where everything and nothing
moves at a different pace.
It's a cosmic revelation
of all I never knew
and no matter which path I take
they all lead back to you.
I know that you would save me
should that tether break,
then transient forever,
never more to wake.

Citrine Trees
Charlene Phare

Sun streaks through the forest
Warm ambience lingers
Kissed by early morning dew
Laying heavy on the ground
Where Citrine trees surround

Autumn is arriving
Leaves slowly changing colour
There's nothing they can do
Nature has full control
Time will take its toll

Every morning returns
Birds sing their songs
Each chirp ringing true
Embrace the great outdoors
Don't put your life on pause

Citrine trees are standing
Against the stunning glow
Where sunlight shines through
Allow your leaves to ebb and flow
Enable eternal love to grow

Spindrift

Gregory Richard Barden

how proper that I found you for
my farewell, midst those dunes
the sands where I did oft adore
your flesh, daubed by the moon

o numberless, the softened eves
those callow hearts would wend
but promises quite often grieve
and swift, would come their end

to press my kiss upon your eye
dove cheek, soft placed a-palm
I bent to meet your sullen sigh
so breathed for kindness' calm

devoutly yours, myself, entire
the draught to draw your wine
you yet devour'd me, eyes afire
white-kneed, before your shrine

my blood as passion, let to be
the sweet sate for your thirst
a fiery flood you then set free
a seed, consumed and cursed

o how's a laurel placed a-brow
this man, so chilled and damned
can bring such deed to thus avow
lost love, wrought on the sand

and tho' I wore a garland, brief
so crowned, for summer's death
our love had withered as a leaf
'midst autumn's flaming breath.

Where Others Saw Chaos, I Saw a Pattern

Patrick Darnell

Dust of language written in tangled letters,
Might they fall off the spheres of stones,
Languid letters enthralling confusion,
But if they fuse with spirit, they enlighten

So far all we see are death cults,
And juggernauts hastily conceded,
And nomenclature of entropy,
And myriads of hypertension

Probably no one knows the script
Or which sacred cow to sacrifice
No, none can mouth proper treatment
Of script, spittle, and spit.

What green fingered paladin will strapple us
To lead us to hills filled with wood duck
And yellow geese, where principia perches
Will it be a messenger paraclete or a hero?

A pattern emerges that bears our burdens
Though not good enough just to recognize it
For it is not a simple understanding, it is
Compelling nomenclature and loaded words

For us living and for us to be living as figures
There are mile posts designated for scrutiny
Leaving stones unturned would be disgraceful
Let's not speak of the end nor tattered remains

Which is going to bring one to term,
Phantom pregnancy or abiogenesis in a womb
No, instead we'll call joy to the cistern
And drink living water to quench the flames.

Deep into the Forest—Run

Sarah Joy Holden

Run long—deep into the forest
Fleeing from all urban space
Feel the beat of a racing heart
Great escape—from all who chase

Run long—deep into the forest
Find yourself a hiding place
Within the trees' beating heart
A place not-one can see

Run long—deep into the forest
Hidden by tree and bracken
From the world—take retreat
Go deeper and further remain

Run long—deep into the forest
From a world of conflict and pain
Hiding between day and the night
Let nature be—ones only companion

Run long—deep into the forest
Where upon—you stumble and fall
Thereby—forever you'll be lost
Because no one ever heard you yell

Run long—long deep into the forest
A moment now turns into ever-after
As hounds find—ones flesh and bone
This forest—becoming your burial plot.

Delayed Reaction
Charlene Phare

Senses hit out of the blue
Something said, yet nothing new
Slowly thoughts penetrate
Second class fuse, feeling irate

Somehow the words have pierced my skin
So I must shut them out, not let them in
Speak to my soul to comfort me
Shock to the system drastically

Somewhere deep down trouble was caused
Sometimes our lives are paused
Seeking subtraction
Suffering from delayed reaction

Silently we will recover
Slow burning flames we can smother
Swamped in self-love constantly
Showing resistance

Never Silent, Never Far Away
Darren Howie

The piper's in the distance
Near the cliff I used to dance
Piping up an invite, drum rolling chance
Dawn gate serenade, on the edge romance
For all the addicts in a trance

The dragon might be tamed
But its fire hasn't waned
Its chasing never ceases as it's
breathing out my name
As it's licking with its flames

The monkey might be off my back
But it's not gone very far
It's swinging in the jungle
With an eerie mocking laugh

The turkey might be free
Running wild among the trees
But it's strutting for attention
Clucking hypertension
Trying to tempt me

The snake it might have lost its bite
Its venom vanished overnight
Still its fangs are being sharpened
Like a dagger piercing knife
In the cave it likes to hide
It's ever prepped and poised to strike

The Mind You Cannot Trust
Darren Howie

I don't trust the mind
For it takes me places I don't want to go
A thousand little chemicals
at war to take control

Cul-de-sacs of crazy
Off road maps
taunting faces
Haunted places
Shadow lands
Motor races
Tangled mass

Memories
Failures
Regrets
And phases
Sleeping giants

Trap doors, mazes

A thousand little chemicals
at war to take control
I don't trust the mind
For it takes me places I don't want to go

The past where the stones of shame strike the soul
Future's where fear runs riot on the beat
Those carved out channels where the chemicals flow
Like ants being attacked as they scutter to and fro

I don't trust the mind
For it takes me places I don't want to go
A thousand little chemicals
at war to take control

It's an enemy of the present
The thief of peace
The pirate of persuasion
The artist of confusion
Or is it the mobster of the deep
Sorry, monster in the street

I don't trust the mind
For it takes me places I don't want to go
A thousand little chemicals
at war to take control

Altered realities
Fatal fatalities
Fictional calamities
As the terror grows

Where fantasy breeds
The illusions feed
The jaded mind
Like a circus show

A thousand little chemicals

at war to take control
I don't trust the mind
For it takes me places I don't want to go

Truth that's bent
Fabricated hells
Twisted facts
To the heart it sells

I don't trust the mind
For it takes me places I don't want to go
A thousand little chemicals
at war to take control
It runs amuck if you let it blow
Conjures chaos if you let it so

The Dance of Death

Lorna McLaren

While out walking in the woods,
where bluebells grew and tall trees stood,
sweet music tantalized his ears
and seemed to draw him ever near
'til whence he saw her through the trees,
where she danced as one with the breeze.
He stood enthralled as she danced around,
naked feet appearing to caress the ground,
hair like spun gold, skin pure as silk,
ne'er before had he seen her ilk.
He wondered if she saw him there
or in her dance she didn't care.
Her beauty took his breath away
and with the music began to sway,
moving closer as the rhythm took hold
he wondered at his being so bold
and unbeknowing of his fate
he joined her dance in trance-like state
as if enchanted by some spell
while listening to his own death knell.

The Seeker
David Catterton Grantz

In the hazy in between
Where all is known but nothing seen,
I drift to somewhere I can't know
In a bayou's gentle flow.

Beside me sails a silver swan
That parts the satin darkling pond;
He croaks for food, he does not wonder
How water holds or breaks asunder.

Oh, my love, we travelled all this way,
Alone, together, for a day,
Hewn from just the sand and clay;
I cannot answer, I can't comprehend
What cannot be seen.

Above me hangs the ancient moss,
The measure of the life I've lost,
The life once taught in crystal glints,
Flown on wings of recompense.

A lone observer drifts in swoons
Of memories from time's cocoon,
As through the trees a milky moon
Dapples shadows into runes.

I know, my love, that life's a mystery,
And that from these spectral trees,
No answer's coming;
Still I seek it, I yearn for it;
I will never turn away from you.

Numbered

Steve Wheeler

Appalling numbers rising falling
bringing base to neutral space
all at sixes and sevens
I traverse the heavens
across the universe
the blazing stars disperse
a galaxy of gravimetric waves
in mathematic levity of graves
of gravity it all subtracts to brevity
and all adds up to sums of parts
by darkest arts of multiplicity
and there it starts in multiple places
of decimal dances
the decadence races
and prances to embrace
a five that comes alive
in horizons of events
through hole-black dents
the numbered line a logic sign
that evermore prevents
A fumbled nine
encumbered time
commenced through
calculated grids of history
presents a mystery in misty sea
gives multi-numbered lists to me.

I sense events that math prevents
the numbers fall equations call
a Fibonacci sequenced crawl
symbolic clash of crash and stall
integrity of integers
with strange parentheses
in ones and twos
of old black shoes that multiply
their soles in news thrown pride

to subjugate and so divide
subtraction satisfaction
of a three-four putrefaction
no reaction just redaction
of a formulaic mis-contraction
count on me or count on that
to calculate a gate of eight
it is a fact you can't go back
to where the opposites attract
so click to get your kicks
and watch your (sixty) six
be vexed, you can't protect a world
from knowing what comes next.

While numbers rise and numbers fall
you figure you won't win them all
the sum of all our conflicts
is the summer of our fall
but that's not all it isn't small
who all the digit counters stall
the obverse universe
becomes a curse
to cause creation's adverse fall
and sharp decline oh number nine
superfluous track, a music crime
white album chime
a miscellaneous rhyme
at number ten the pigs in pens
pass legislation yet again
they number with the grey old men
and circle the overlap like Venn
but when oh when will violence bend
ad infinitum is the trend
when will these numbers
reach their numbing end?

Sand Paper

James Kenny

This house is a house full of sand.
It invades the cracks, inundates the crevices,
infects the wrinkles of my skin.
Grinding, grinning,
eroding everything it touches,
wood smooth, flesh raw,
a paradox of application.

Each room is half filled with it,
hourglass high,
Passageways like ochre trenches
mark the common ground.
A fever of stingrays pass by the window
a sea born memory of flight,
of light, crackling, electric.

In the dull lit hallway,
a crooked bookcase.
Sand-bound volumes,
destructive to each other,
never opened, never read,
parched paper yellows tooth-like,
toothless ideas crumble,
dust to dust, rust to rust,
misbegotten and forgotten
The boiling waves erode the rocks,
splitting and spitting a granular conversation.
Dredged memory crushed microscopic,
sand castles, sand bags,
sand the size of sauros worlds,
it lays in the ignored corners of your room,
Swept neatly, nearly, imperfectly, clean.

Weeping Woman
Joseph Gallagher

The 'weeping woman' was me, though I never wept
Only inside and only while I slept.
The painting unto this late day haunts, a bitter ghost
A coven of teeth chattering, insecure, inept...
Pinned to history this house frau floats.

The cringing crying face, fat sausage fingers linger
Clamped to the chin, waiting to be devoured.
The hour of sorrow and unforgiveness was upon us.
All camouflaged by carnival colors, festooned
By flowers and foolishness, party hats for harpies.

I, who walked you to the door of Guernica
And pushed you through, imploring the deities —
The gods of war to birth this painting you ignored —
I gave you my eyes that saw the light in you
Which you transfigured to shadow and stone.

I gave you my song like a river and sang you to sleep.
You turned my voice to mud, my eyes to weep.
I gave you the moonlight, extravagant excess
Of irresistible desire. You painted deserts and thorns.

I gave you the wings of my dreams so that you could feel
The gossamer images drifting over your corneas
Like the trail of a silken wedding dress —
You gave me back bedlam, curses, omens a hex.

I gave you dances on the sands of sensual beaches.
I gave you the fire that glows under my skirt —
The candle wax wetness that clings to my thighs,
My arched back like the waves breaking under thundering
skies.

Now I gather the nothingness you left me
Like a shawl of red roses around my shoulders.
I wrap the moonlight in wax paper — take it to go.

—

I strip love from my long delicate fingers shorn
Like discarded gloves, their season gone.

When The Seagulls Cried
Susan Ila Davis

When the seagulls cried
they cried for me.
I couldn't bring the tears to my eyes
They had to help me see

We together, no more close.
Tilt my glass for another dose
Of reality.

You always stared at the others
So we glared at one another.
Until I turned away

Then my flesh so ready and yours
My heart was open, when it poured.
Empty and ignored.

Gone were the days of a lingering kiss
I take away what you will miss.
Remains turn to dust.

Waves crash , seagull noises
They cried for us.
Sound effects in between empty voices
You never grieved the trust.

When the seagulls cried
they cried for me,
Soared the ever changing sky.
Helped set my hurt heart free.

Infinite Suspense

Sharon Toner

I yearn to see all that you are
The endless hours of your life already spent
To traverse the passageways of your mind
To linger there a while in infinite suspense

I yearn to see all that you are
The endless days of your life already spent
To traverse the emotions of your sacred heart
To linger there a while in infinite suspense

I yearn to see all that you are
The endless months of your life already spent
To traverse the enlightenment of your spirit
To linger there a while in infinite suspense

I yearn to see all that you are
The endless years of your life already spent
To traverse the whole of your entire being
To linger there a while in infinite suspense.

In My Mind

Victoria Puckering

In my mind
Imagination is mine
Yet, you are so defined
As pixels get in line
A picture of humankind
— — — — — — — — — — — — — —
A picture of humankind
As pixels get in line
Yet, you are so defined
Imagination is mine
In my mind

Peace of Mind
Gordon Horton

I've been a lot of places
And I've done a lot of things
I've loved a lot of women
Sometimes losses come with stings
The time is growing closer
My decision has been made
I'll no longer punch a time clock
I've already made the grade
I'll wake up when I want to
Spend my nights with one I love
Listen to the wind speak
With the voices from above
My new calling won't be graded
By the standards most must meet
I'll tell the world a story
One I'm yearning to complete
I've others that need work
And a rhyme or two inside
There's tons of things for me to do
Though some I haven't tried
I'll soon go to see my brother
In the land of Dreadlock Larry
Check that off my bucket list
A week or so we'll tarry
Just a few more weeks of labor
Running hard to stay in place
Until I can break the chain
That keeps me bound to run this race
I have to say I'll miss the work
Of bringing things folks need
But I'll not miss the microscope
I'm under with each deed
With the Spring will come a time
When once more I will find
The lonesome voices on the wind
That bring me Peace of Mind

Embraced by Autumn
Brandon Adam Haven

Embraced by Autumn's resplendent caress
Dissolving into naught, my whispers softly sigh
I exhale ethereal breath, the crispness doth refresh

Within the day of a fading leaf's distress
Stripped of its verdant vigor, it shall now die
Embraced by Autumn's resplendent caress

In transparency hued, its fleeting tale doth suppress
Bedight in russet vestments, a wistful cry
I exhale ethereal breath, the crispness doth refresh

The zephyrs pirouette, a melancholic mess
A sound of rustling, as days race by
Embraced by Autumn's resplendent caress

Through the amber twilight's veil, I must confess
I seek to intertwine life's transient dye
I exhale ethereal breath, the crispness doth refresh

With solemn reverence, I trace this evanescent essence
This ebbing beauty bids a transient goodbye
Embraced by Autumn's resplendent caress
I exhale ethereal breath, the crispness doth refresh

Only Pain Knows Full the Sweetness
David Catterton Grantz

Only pain knows full the sweetness
As new tendrils come to light,
A warming balm, caress of breezes,
As wind dancers cross to night.

Your tender heart can find no reason;
Your mind abides its amber bruise,
Like ocean storms dislodging boulders,
In grief so deep we'd never choose.

Don't embrace forever heartache,
Always mind the budding rose;
No matter paths a lonesome heart takes,
Its shadows flow from where light goes.

I have arms to hold you closer
And ears to listen to your cries;
I'll build a mighty bridge if you'll let me
Stream through prisms in your eyes.

The End
Lorna McLaren

Something stole the stars last night,
removed them from the sky,
the moon was left so desolate
he blinked out with just a sigh.
The darkness in his element
shrouded all around,
devouring everything in sight
and all without a sound.
Silence spoke a thousand words
but none that we could hear,
a deep foreboding took their place,
I fear the end is near!

North Wind Blows

Amanda Wilson

Within the forest when the north wind blows
the boughs of the trees offer no succour,
the bitter wind whips, clouds open and close.

The evergreen shakes and so falls the snow,
unseen animals, all undercover.
Within the forest when the north wind blows.

Holly and ivy glance from the hedgerow,
no protection bared, over exposure.
The bitter wind whips, clouds open and close.

Mammals hibernate, digging a burrow,
sleeping all winter hidden in armour.
Within the forest when the north wind blows.

A snowstorm ensues, a blizzard? Who knows?
No colour to speak of, white each contour.
The bitter wind whips, clouds open and close.

Trudging through the forest, no drift shallow.
Clouds threatening bad weather to follow.
within the forest when the north wind blows,
the bitter wind whips, clouds open and close.

Candy Floss Hills

Gemma Tansey

The clouds are made of chewing gum
The sea is made of milk
The people made of plasticine
The beach is made of silk

Chocolate rivers with biscuit boats
Go sailing down the stream
Where marsh-mellow ducks paddle along
And everyone seems in a dream

The cars are made of tropical fruit
The houses are made of cake
The pets are made of play-dough
Their smells you can't mistake

Rainbow puddles from rainbow rain
Dry up in a matter of seconds
Candy-floss hills surround the view
The smell of sweet honey it beckons

The sun shines brighter than gold
The birds sing loud and proud
The people all have blue eyes
And they live on a silver lined cloud

Peace reigns freely in all the towns
And everyone you meet is so calm
Love and laughter fill the air
And no-one ever comes to harm

The wind blows gently and always warm
The air is as clear as glass
The silk white beaches line the shores
The milk sea is calm and so vast

Orchard fruit trees line all the streets
And the smell invigorates the senses

All is tranquil and nothing is rushed
Your mind has no need for defences

The streets are paved with platinum
The roads are smooth and not rough
The cars all run off CO2
And love? There is always enough

The air is clear and ok to breath
The people are all so healthy
The atmosphere is one of peace
And affection it renders them wealthy

So close your eyes and picture it now
Allow yourself the dream
Can you imagine what it would be like
In a life made of plasticine

Drunk

A.B. Dawn

drunk
cigarette in hand
she totters to me and the world
which had just slipped off her hands
is on free fall
like a supreme void she descends next to me
in a mountainous step
in her eyes the hidden stars go up one after another
she stretches towards me a palm
like all the Martian deserts yet unmapped
she asks for a lighter
I give her all the fire
and my soul.

The Flood
Sarah Wheatley Tillbrook

Rain, the essence of a soul
Trickles down below God's eyelids
When His earth is bare of gold
Tears feel down, colour from iris
Water wash into the soil
Bringing up the colours, fresh
For all His pain, the work the toil
Tears repair the mortal flesh

No Rescue
Sharon Toner

I need no rescue today
I've moved on from yesterday
Like the flow of the sea
And the wind that blows over me
I'll go with the ebb and flow
For time always knows
Just when to tug at your elbow
Bringing you back to reality
With all its idiosyncrasies
So I'll just unlock the door
Revealing what's at my core
For I have just simple dreams
I don't need manic extremes
So I'll let the tide now turn
Letting myself return
To the peacefulness within
And the sound of my internal violin
For every note it plays
Undoes any kind of malaise
Until I transcend all life's noise
Once again regaining my poise.

Emptiness
Crispulo Tapa

Emptiness permeates
the blank space
Like words that are devoid
of any meaning
Wandering thoughts like
hazy clouds
That though heavy brings
no real rain.

The heart palpitates yet
feels no pain
Empty of emotions like
an empty train
Running thru an open
and long rail
Brings no reason why
it should stay.

The emptiness in our
worldly lives
Has given many a man
so much pain
Though rich with earthly
material gains
Feels a deep void, an
emptiness within
Seeks the pleasures of
life, be entertained.

Yet there is that emptiness
like a shadow
That follows even when
he is sleepin'
A ghost that hounds,
keeping him awake
Until he begins

dreaming of a life fulfilled
But was never realized,
'twas just a dream.

Until he found the love of a
God he almost forgot
Where there was once an
emptiness within
Now it's filled with joy and
love only God can give.

Indefinitely
Scot A. Buffington

Be well assured, you own this heart
and every pulse inside the chest
no human will, shall every part
nor still it past eternal rest.

Our sleepless souls may carry on
a love that glows to spite the grave
they knew before, in lives bygone
embraced and took far less than gave.

These tragic woes to suffer fate
when one departs to wander free
the other left to pine, await
born again, indefinitely.

Instruct the guides, our two, old ghosts
each turn we take in bodies, fresh
though temporary, gorgeous hosts
true love is not confined to flesh.

First Love, Old Orchard Beach Maine
Joseph Gallagher

That last summer with a thousand Julys
Nothing mattered but the moment
And the endless nights...
The sun's crazy blue bright weather
Like a young man's hands electric with want.

The wind above convertibles sighed
In the brilliant silver soft sky.
The stars were stars and the moon ached
In its own translucent heaven—
His thirst for living could not be slaked

He was the king of the path a train whistle cut
Crazy for speed, he held the girl and the wheel
And plunged toward the ocean lands where the squeal
Of seagulls and the smell of salt sprayed air
Mingled with neon and fog drifting over the bar
By the boardwalk caressing the night like a soft kiss...
I remember this...

And summer let me sing the songs
I swore I'd never forget.
That summer, that last summer of week long nights
Blossom dark, fragrant with wild flowers and dew,
And a dust as fine as milled flour...
Summer let me sleep for hours
Until closed gauze curtains let daylight through—

I woke with the scent of my girl around me,
Clinging to me as the ocean clings to blue
Remembering the night before...
Slick with sweat, flesh blooming fluids
Like a liquid Garden of Eden.

The turntable played muted Motown,
While I sang of a loss I could barely imagine
Of broken hearts I could barely believe.

The world rode shotgun and reclined like beauty
On the seat of my car, lovely in the glow
From the dashboard lights...
Rapt inside the infinite night —
And I knew what it meant to adore.

Summer let me dawdle there,
On the precipice of becoming.
And for a moment, poised there
Listening to the summer night breathe
And the soul sounds on the radio,
Everything seemed possible...
Love without loss, life without heartbreak
Seemed perfectly plausible.

Beyond the Mirage
Lora Lee

I'm stumbling upon this silken labyrinth in my mind,
Where thoughts, like moths, flutter and intertwine,
There lies a darkness, dense and profound,
Yet, within it, my true self is often found.

I dance around it, in elegant prose,
Hoping to disguise what deep down, one knows.
But when I dare to delve, to truly see,
It's there I find my raw, unfiltered reality.

Not in the shimmering mirage of dreams,
But in the quiet corners, where the shadows gleam.
It's not the external that makes me whole,
Instead, it's the introspective journey of my soul.

Accepting the facets, the pain, the glee,
Unveils the person I'm destined to be

food paste
Matt Elmore

no schools, no tools; nowhere to learn
no placation, no station, no money to burn...
no doctors or groceries, no transportation
no protection, no medicine, only frustration
no movie shows with very little clothes ...

entire families with no sanitation
no smart phones or form of satiation
only a small taste of food paste
and one sweet prayer of meditation...

it's hard to consider, in our world of plenty
it's only our world... not a world of so many...
our foolish complaining, made in haste
try that complaining, when all you have to eat
... is food paste...

A Moonlight Sea
Victoria Puckering

A moonlight sea
Brings treasures on the surreal beach
Within my reach
Perfect shells complement the pearls of the sea
Held in shell clasp
Nature adapts
As a moving wave is held in place
In a rock of sea glass
Translucent and held in time
As I grasp
A moment in history
A thousand years to mould
Like a trinket box forever enclosed
The moving wave stood still
Like a picture in an old camera film

I Wonder What a Dog Thinks
Richard Harvey

I wonder what a dog thinks when you're sitting on the can
I wonder what a dog thinks when you try to shake its hand
I wonder what a dog thinks when you're watching your TV
I wonder what a dog thinks when they look at you and me

I wonder what a dog thinks when you're talking on the phone
I wonder what a dog thinks when you leave them all alone
I wonder what a dog thinks when they see you fuss and fight
I wonder what a dog thinks when you turn out all the lights

I wonder what a dog thinks that makes them so faithful to you
I wonder what a dog thinks when you are feeling blue
I wonder what a dog thinks when you're mad and yell at them
I wonder what a dog thinks that makes him man's closest friend
And I wonder why a dog would choose to be man's closest friend

Quantum Entanglement
Lora Lee

Atoms dance, delicate and free,
Quantum threads weaving destiny.
No accidents, only shades of light,
Spun by gaze, defining night.
Vast expanses where truths contend,
Probabilities rise, shift, and bend.
Observer's focus shapes the flow,
Crafting existence, making it so.
What seems random, mere twist of fate,
Quantum tales a different relate.
Each moment, both early and late,
Our sight seals open or locks the gate.
The universes ballet, constantly spun,
Perception's power creates the sun.

Life in the City
Lucille LaRoche

The deep indigo night
sprinkles a mizzling rain
on the heat parched
city streets
The summer heat wave
permeates its environ
you can almost hear the
city's sighs of relief
The walkers of the night
at their own robotic pace
welcome its refreshing
touch on their sweltering skin
A summer breeze,
finding its own path
between narrow spaces
of statuesque buildings
soothing an encapsulated
city of man-made buildings
of steel and concrete now
sparse of trees from long ago
Street lights appear like stars
and the lights within
tall buildings appear like the
constellations of a night sky
Reflections of the night
paint their colored nuances
on moist city streets 'a
for a vision of the walkers
of the night' while many
are fast asleep —
They know their city Streets
as their shadows and imprints
of the night will remain unseen
within the solitude of the night
without a trace

Dear Mama

Gregory Richard Barden

dear Mama, have you found that other side
where loved ones, hope and heaven all reside?
oh do you stroll, Dad's hand lost deep in yours
and breathe the splendid air, that kingdom's shores?

dear Mama are you dancing with your knight
in sturdy armor, that you shined so bright?
oh do you paint new landscapes of that realm
and sail those azure seas, Dad at the helm?

dear Mama are you singing bright and clear
and sharing anecdotes to charm or cheer?
oh are you with your dear ones who have passed?
so many went before you, far too fast.

dear Mama, do you know how much I miss
our talks and nature walks, your loving kiss?
oh do you yearn our sweet connection, rare
that even without words, was always there?

dear Mama do you know the hole that now
I have to heal within my heart somehow?
oh what's this man to do, his mama gone
but for her sake, find ways to carry on?

dear Mama I will spread your love for life
the grace and care you gave as mom and wife
I'll do my best to share my heart, like you
your smile deep inside, to get me through

dear Mama, death has taken such a toll
still, I've one hope, eternal, for my soul
that someday when my body sets it free
dear Mama's open arms … will wait for me.

In Faith

Farha Abbasi

I believe and I doubt
What if I was the rain
That drench thirsty souls
and remain parched
What if I am a vessel
that sail the wayward souls
Home remains forever lost

What if I am the heart
that pours love
On weary and broken
stay shattered into small pieces
What if the purpose is to
Fulfil others
stay empty and forever seeking

What if the destination is
to find solace in pain
Be the giving tree stand-alone
Bear the scorching sun
So others can thrive
Live in its shade
Be the rhythm
Everyone dance to
And never harmonize

I doubt but also believe
In an unfolding tomorrow
Where doubts be buried
faith stands supreme
I doubt yet I believe…

Last Embers
Donna Smith

Wrestling to stay with me, the embers flicker with hope,
Their freedom celebrated in their dance.
Whispering a sweet hypnotic rhapsody,
A longing and desire to escape and elope.

Captivated within the flare of the rainbow fire,
I sit motionless in the dwam before slumber.
Their perpetual swaying has me transfixed,
The motion soporific in its entire.

As the last embers of the fire fade, fighting to stay,
A cool breeze blows in, and I let it find me.
It tickles my skin as it strokes and caresses,
While the enduring flames perform their last ballet.

Every Day I Drill for Gold
J.T. Caine

every day i drill for gold
but it's never really found
only a black sludge comes
up through the muddy ground
no veins of shiny silver
nor diamonds in the stones
only ink with which i think
there's a story in my bones
so from this moment onward
i will blacken the white page
with the sludge from my head
and escape this tiny cage

The Brontë Sisters

Jessica Ferreira Coury Magalhães

People whose faces I'll never know
Are the ones who intrigue me the most.
Three shadows in a row
But their features are a blur.

Pacing around a table
Going up and down the stairs
Many have the mind of a genius
But never as sharp as theirs.

Ink, paper and pen
Pretending they were three men
They didn't even know then
Their mere existence was an event.

People whose faces I'll never see
Their likeness painted by an amateur
Who did not appreciate at the proper degree
The luck he had to share their same earth.

Three figures on the heath
Three skirts ruffling like angel wings
Three souls bustling underneath
Three spirits onto the paper spring.

People whose faces I'll never know
Pacing on the rails of my mind
The past won't open its curtains to show
What I can only dream of as I type.

Awaken

Christopher Mercon

I watch the year struggle
into immortality
where spring would burgeon like a child,

to softly wade into the
summer's maturity
where autumn's splendid colors smiled.

Just to fall into the grip of winter
into the course where death
would seem to win

to the point where new
life's spring would enter —
awaken dear, we must try
this again.

I led life toward
all that I should be
unto the time where death
would yet set in;

life's clarion call
clearly came to me —
awaken dear, we must
try this again.

Vampire
J Henry DeKnight

To all the living things
I tell you how life sings
Oldest guy at work
Set amongst the young new hires
Showing wisdom often
Like in the movies …
I'm an ageless vampire
Having lived so many lives
have the answers for most equations
being called on to perform
solving problems on all occasions
To all the living things
I tell how life sings
Clocks they chime and bells
they ring clearer working
moonlight to moonlight
with no reflection in the mirror…

Life May Not Be Fair
Richard Harvey

You know life may not be fair, but it's good
It may not turn out the way you thought it would
You can live life or forsake it
But it's exactly what you make it

You know life may not be fair, but it's all we got
And it really doesn't matter if you like that or not
It's up to you if you're miserable or kind
That all depends on your state of mind

You know life may not be fair, but too bad
It's time to stop complaining and feeling sad
You know you're the master of your own estate
You're the only one to blame for the life you make

———

If Only I had the Time
Victoria Puckering

At least one time
I wish I could rewind
Travelling back in time
To replay hot summer days
As cold snowflakes fall
Has someone pressed fast forward?
It is next year in no time
I wish I could rewind
If only I had the time

If only I had the time
I wish I could rewind
It is next year in no time
Has someone pressed fast forward?
As cold snowflakes fall
To replay hot summer days
Travelling back in time
I wish I could rewind
At least one time

Written to Death
Dara C. Vazquez

My love hurts.

Its pain
written by fingers
quilled to sharp points,
recklessly dipped,
into the soft spaces
of a wounded heart.

Pressed mercilessly,
memories traced in vain.
Splattered heedlessly,
with no regard to shame.

Blank paper
wraps itself around four chambered walls
permanently stained
packaged and delivered.
To be forgotten.

And yet these fingers continue to stab.
Until the inkwell dries,
shrivels and dies.
My hands' evidence,
of my heart's own massacre.

Overlap
Gavin Prinsloo

There is a place where reality and illusion meet,
where the distinction is blurred,
and where words are slurred.

A place devoid of logic or dream,
where the tangible and the intangible flows;
where it goes, no one knows.

There is a place of misty form,
where eyes are open but do not see,
a place of confluence that reason dictates,
really should not be.

Hands feel but do not touch,
spatial anomalies exist where none should be;
there is no life here, no limb not tree.

It exists, it truly must,
this place of nothing and everything,
this place where imagination goes to die;
I see it clearly, here, no bird can fly.

Emotions of Love

Lokanath Rath

When I see smile in your visage
It brings me the feelings of morning
That asks me to read the hidden message
Which will bring my soul serene.

When I face your rage
It reminds me the afternoon sun's oppression
My soul cries for the freedom from the bonding's cage
Which may end this problem in our relation.

When I see your sad face
That reminds me the pains of dusk
My thoughts start to read it along with time's race
Silently I wait for the questions you will ask.

When I see your calmness
That reminds me about evening
Who waits for the moon's caresses
This imbues my feelings.

When I look into your eyes
It reminds me the darkness of the night
Who hides the pains and waits to cry
This brings my soul plight.

When I see in your eyes tears
It reminds me the dawn's cry and dews
Both remain silent, but want to do whispers
My soul wants to paint them with love's hue

Love is the Most Twisted Curse of All

Hussaini Bukar

Love is as beautiful as flowers
And is as dangerous as venom
Once a thought, booked a heart
Many a good, suffers
and enjoys its tune
It depends on whom you choose
and how you fight for it

For centuries a thought, finest to sieve
Love is a magical tune of mighty power
Subtle, sublime and arrows strike
As rich as it is, its curse
bleeds and melts clad

Oh! For many a times,
I put up a question
If love is the right answer to happiness
Why many suffer from it
cure as diseases
But neither my view,
rather to my fight

I meant to status love as illusion
For being a philosopher
as righteous as to cough
Love is just a hard bitten era
In others' face not as all as to judge
I plead to conscience the flag

A Soulful Rapture
Linda Falter

Awesome in beauty
Nature's front door
Always leaving us
Wanting for more...

Sunlight filtering
Through ghost like trees
Heartbeats flutter
Like buzzing bees...

Feelings we get
From dampness of dew
Meadows of flowers
Skies of blue...

Within us all
A soulful rapture
Seeking to find
Entice and capture...

Feelings we get
Inspiring and true
The way I feel
When I hold you...

Awesome in beauty
Nature's front door
Always leaving us
Wanting for more...

Bosom of the Storm
Rafik Romdhani

The first wave of love
splashes over graves
deserted by life.

Dawn, like the kissed
face of a bartendress,
ventures into the night.

Gently comes in the light
and breaks the cups
brimming with darkness.

Your eye widely opens
for the bosom of a storm
like a sky for two wings.

The first wave of love
jumps out like all emotions
and never returns to its ocean.

Kintsugi
Tom Cleary

Cracks, breaks in crazed cups
fissures, fragments of pain
desolation of separation
shattered in eggshell chips
the hard rocks of regret resound.

But you, the phoenix of life
pluck your own feather
apply the gold seams of a dawn
now blazing in my chest
a soothing scintillation
where the glaze of your gaze
is my strength.

I Lost My Heart a Time Ago

Valerie Dohren

I lost my heart a time ago,
it silently took flight —
I looked within the daylight hours,
and in the dark of night.

I searched amidst the golden leaves
of autumn, cast around,
then glanced upon the glist'ning stars
which there above abound.

And here amongst the tangled vines,
along the wooded ways,
I yearned to hear its gentle throb
through many endless days.

I sought it in the crystal snow,
and deep in feathered wings.
Amongst sweet-scented lavender,
and all soft tender things.

In silver streams and leafy glens,
bathed in the twilight's glow,
to find my heart and feel it beat
as once a time ago.....

To find my heart and feel it beat
as once a time ago.

Asking for a Friend

Steve Wheeler

Can this world ever be at peace?
How will the troubles ever cease?
Can we bring conflict to an end?
I'm asking — for a friend

Who will wipe the tear drops dry?
When will dark clouds flee the sky?
Will the heartbreaks ever mend?
I'm asking — for a friend

Who will tend to broken hearts?
Who'll stop trouble before it starts?
Who'll find out where freedom went?
I'm asking — for a friend

Who will take the lonely nights
Turn them into sheer delights
The One on whom I can depend
I'm asking for a friend

Inklings

Eric Aguilar

Can you hear
the word? It's calling you
In open spine and chord.
Fleece the pen till it seeps inklings
upon the geography of the mind.
Wines in clay vessels aging over time,
lines on paper; my utensil a pencil to scribe.
Sentences of stimulation-provoking synapses
sparking neurons compete of rise and collapse.

The Endless Nothing
Dale Parsons

As seas stretch out into endless nothing
So too will our slumber in death
The winds they coax our sail a luffing
The bite and the sting of its breath

As the shoreline long ago did fade
So too will our time on this world
The boat and crew though sturdy made
Now the twain, appearance burled

As the sun and moon cast down their gaze
A contemplated fate, we wait to see
Will they conclude to end our days
The boat did its best...did we?

As shadow falls on our final day
So too the sail will cease a luffing
May tales of our deeds endure to stay
As we enter the endless nothing

In Spite
Imelda Zapata Garcia

Beyond a setting Sun, despite Lunar eclipse,
above the shroud of darkness
a glowing ember lifts
Though thunder shuts down Stars
while deluge drapes their sparks
a radiant flame does dare
to dazzle right on through
For gods lie in wait, to stroke
a heart ablaze
and stumble in our wake
and trip the light fantastic
that yours be splendorous haze

Nature's Voice
Donna Smith

Hush now she whispered as the breeze floated past,
Breathe in the silence, allow this moment to last.
Take a seat by my riverbank, inhale the fresh air,
Dip your toes in my water and let down your hair.
Take a walk through my garden, smell all the sweet flowers,
Drink in the aroma, let your senses devour.
Stroll through my forests, let each season entrance,
Skip through every meadow, in exuberant dance.
Sail all of my oceans, into their watery depths,
Take in their calmness, travel every inch, width, and breath.
Look up to the sky and watch the birds soar,
Tread over my land, discover, explore.
Let the wind take you onwards, let the stars be your guide,
The world in its entirety, appreciate all I provide

On the Aft Deck
Patricia Garner

You were sleeping with
a smile stretching
Like the crescent moon
The rising and falling
Hand over your heart
Pledging to the stars
When your lips parted
As if expecting to find
The matching pair
Of closed eyes
You sighed
I wanted to surprise you
With a kiss transcendent
As I watched you and
daydreamed
As you dreamt

Our Souls at Night

James Martin

While drifting out the window on
a starry summer night....
I glanced on back to see me there
in softened amber light.

Slumbering relentlessly,
I drifted slowly away
to the lightest spews of dust there
to mingle in their spray.

Away from me....away...away
so high above treetops....
the wind is my lover whisking me far.
She never stops.

She carries me all through the night
to stars in gleeful dance.
Naked I fly through the dawn
in inebriated trance.

Once more my soul in regretful plunge,
blinded by the bright
rejoins me with such lofty
aspirations of delight.

And visions of escape into tomorrow's
night-time flee...
far...far from this tired worn out body...
once more...to be free.

no reply dragonfly
Matt Elmore

no reply dragon fly
my skeletal remains
imply accusation's pains
with wings too weak too wide
too withdrawn to comply
no reply for this dragonfly

no height for respite
nor shelter for rains
or dangerous games
in survival behind eyes
contrived beyond any prize …
even for dragonflies

breathing fireflies fighting ice
in freezing seasons now blame
actions all tamed the same
a trial upon my demise
convicted of my own cries
answering to such pesky jibes

no reply dragonfly
a sting of reflected flame
kindle a spirit that strains
avoiding all spite
I fly high but never out of sight
no reply for this dragonfly

World Upon Worlds
Lora Lee

They witness but fragments, mere shadows of me,
Glimpses in the physical, what the eye can see.
Yet, unbeknownst, within lies a universe vast,
Extraordinary places, from the first breath to the last.

This inner universe , woven by a timeless love,
Wordless, unbound, like the skies above.
Not to be named, nor held in worldly grasp,
It's the essence, the soul, in each breath, I gasp.

When humanity's chaos seeks to cloud my view,
The divine within gently breaks through.
Knocking softly upon my heart's silent door,
Dispelling the shadows, the doubts it bore.

With clarity, it whispers of beauty so pure,
My truth, unmarred, eternally secure.
In this sacred space, I find my serene,
The unseen depths of being, rarely seen.

Return to Flanders Field
Gregory Richard Barden

old brittle bones are like this fence, so built
   on throes of horrors shrouded with the hilt
   of war's inanely senseless blade, now dulled
   by all the precious souls its edge has culled ...

now ages gone, those boys amid their dreams
   and yet the air still trembles with their screams
   so daubed in bleeding sun, how death imparts
   these fields of poppy roods and purple hearts.

Fields of Green Velvet
Valerie Dohren

Lay me down gently in fields of green velvet
Resting beneath the blue gossamer sky
Where I may gaze upon clouds of white cotton
Shimmering dragonflies floating on by

Mingling there amongst red satin petals
Yellow and silver, with gold all around
Captured by nature's soft breath-taking beauty
Gracing the heavens, adorning the ground

There shall I tarry in peaceful devotion
Breathing the fresh and sweet pine-scented air
Feeling the warmth of the sun cast around me
Free from all worry and heartache and care

Come, won't you join me, to feel all this splendour
There in your mind where such fantasies dwell
Dance with me, sing with me, and then surrender
Each of your cares, and fall under my spell

Kenosis
Iain Strachan

Emptied himself of selfish desires
Laid down his supernatural powers
Absolved the hate of scornful liars
Emptied himself of selfish desires
Zeroed the lust for vengeful fires
Atonement made, forgiveness flowers
Emptied himself of selfish desires
Laid down his supernatural powers

Life's a Hoax

J.T. Caine

I pull on clothes
        I put on shoes
I go outside
        And bring the blues
I wake up early
        I stay up late
I pay the bills
        And somnambulate
I drive around
        I get stuff done
I buy some gas
        And I'm undone
I work all day
        I cook a meal
I watch TV
        And forget to feel
I brush my teeth
        I wash my face
I read a book
        And I'm out of place
I greet my friends
        I call my folks
I do all the things
        And life's a hoax

The Fear of Silence
Martin Gedge

Deep behind
These hollow eyes
Dark as pitch
And stitched with lies
To hang around
A feast of flies
That ties
This broken soul
For hurt
In chain
It shall remain
The mark of choice
A voice in flame
To burn with spit
With grit and grain
To stain
The pain I know
For fear
And hate
Beyond this gate
I'm sure that those
Can all relate
For what you see
Or tolerate
Debate my state as well
For silent still
This evil mill
To push the pin
And pop the pill
There is no time
To find and fill
The thrill or will to tell
For of thy skin
What harbours in

From flesh and bone
Of stone and gin
Prepare to take it
On the chin
To spin this grin I hide
Through lock and key
I fancy thee
Not what you bought
Or thought of me
But true to form
And born to be
This storm to brew inside…

Precipitation
David Catterton Grantz

The rain decided not to fall,
Since it wasn't rain at all.
It puffed around the sky 'til dawn
Then set a bonfire, and was gone.

The snowflakes opted not to swirl —
That they'd not ride Godiva's curls;
It wasn't that they'd formed too late,
But that they, so dainty, must sublimate.

The hail consented not to pound
The rooftops targets 'round the town;
Their stones, swept in the howling draft,
Donned another icy coat, fore-and-aft.

What doesn't come is seldom glimpsed,
And when it does, comes unconvinced.

Reminisce and Renew
Terry Bridges

Memories drip into pools of dreams.
A recreated past where love is kind.
So much torment and heartache we suffer,
Then focus. Seek and you will find.

A quiet place for passion re-assessed,
Unravelling the thread of our lives.
Braving the labyrinthine obstacles,
Fate scissors us through with knives.

The scales of justice gravitate to one side.
No one is ever perfectly in balance.
Typhoons sail through us like the wind,
But purity shields us from malice.

Safe harbour, docking where we started from,
Eternal recurrence. The dawn emerges.
A smudge of light on a far horizon,
Painting with colour the dark's edges.

What new delight awaits its birth.
The brilliant sun slowly arises.
Fortune favours every adventure,
The promised morning pregnant with surprises.

The Problem with Rubies
Jessica Ferreira Coury Magalhães

Man with a long, blue beard
Selling earrings to me
The green one, and the one with navy beads
Both with the pearls hanging.

Bought none of the red things
You see, the problem with rubies
Clear as they may be
Is they remind you that you can bleed.

The pearls, on the contrary
Remind you of smiling teeth
Or happy tears on your cheek
They're more cheerful than the rubies.

Walked around all the city
With new jewels on my ears
One pair for my friend, and one for me
I lost the earrings and the friendship.

Broken Watch
Charlene Phare

As the ticking slowed
Time came to a halt
Still, the backlight glowed
As the ticking slowed
Yet, both hands flowed
My watch had a fault
As the ticking slowed
Time came to a halt

Every Time You Go
Cindy Pagia

Every time you go,
Miles away from me,
Your tear-filled face glows.
I wish I had your mind's key.

In the fog of your head,
How can I follow?
I just sit here and pretend.
Drowning in your sorrow.

I take your hand in mine.
I look you in the eyes
Hoping to see a sign,
A flicker, a light.

But all I see is doubt,
Wonder and surprise!
A stranger, I can't live without.
Saddened by the cloud in your eyes.

Each time you wander off
into your own tortured thoughts,
How do I get through your wall,
To bring you back if you get lost.

Kind
Becky Tee

They said she was crazy
Stood out from the crowd
That she was manic
Distasteful and loud

They said she was shy
Never cared to join in
As though her shyness
Were a mortal sin

They said she was fat
She had 'let herself go'
That she took comfort in food
Incapable of saying no

They said she was skinny
Conceited and vain
Maybe she starves herself?
Self-obsession to blame

She looked in the mirror
Knew she'd never really win
This world can be judgemental
But what matters, is within

She could be anything she liked
As long as she was kind
And that is how she resolved
To be truly defined

When
A.B. Dawn

when life is a blur
the days so similar
they pass before they arrive
the happy minutes slip by
with the lightness of kisses not meant.
when your existence feels like a hiccup
as if it's missing a step

or several
on your way to now.
as if a child blinked twice
before the ice cream stand
and woke up thirty years later
before a mirror in somebody's morning
trying to introduce himself
to the husk glaring back
never knowing where to begin
or when . . .

Finis
Scot A. Buffington

eviscerated well upon a many bladed knife
forged by nimble cursing of a multifaceted past
partook encounters often to extinguish further life
lest fate alone be escort for the instants left to last

heavy handed hearting bore fine apathies of shame
caused incessant riots where the hole should teem with guilt
compromised a reckoning with existential blame
upon a quarried psyche where a better man was built

burned the burdens brightly sprinkled soft upon the pyre
lain as gentle artifacts to souvenir no more
consumed as holy hosting every morsel labelled ire
haunts no longer longings for a death begot from gore

interred beside a healing hope the ceremony blade
fatal dredged a furrow driven fathoms deepest sword
quickened ghosting ignorant what lesser gods forbade
done in the sacred silence of unnecessary word

Swiped
Stephanie Morrow

I swiped so fast it just caught my eye
My anxiety crept up
With an uneven sigh
As I scrolled past this pic
I thought I was sick
Was it supposed to be hid?

But I can't be sure if I saw it or not
Maybe I needed to see another shot
But gone to the vast black screen it went
My fingers too fast, and I had not meant
To swipe so quickly in this game of fools
As I am lost to the usefulness of this devilish tool.

I Do Not Do Tears
Mike Absalom

And yet on this stunning day
the world around appears motionless enough.
Apart from the breeze, time has stopped.
Close to the event horizon I too am stunned.
It seems I am already short of breath.

There was sun and a bitter cold.
And now rain comes, great splashing tears
across the wet autumn leaves that cloak the path.
I do not do tears. I do not do tears.
I leave that to the sky.
But when there is a death in the family
there is a death in the family,
But I do not do tears.

and the moon shone
John Lyons

dear enchanted poetess
i am truly transcended by you
for the wisdom in your words
has duly amended you to
the fog of my marsh
the wind in my reed
my cries for the plight
the blindness and greed
it darkens our souls
turns tinsel our gold
a dirge tale to heed
a world's end foretold

yet we hold fast the light
taste deep the sweet fruit
your heart beat of right
your life breath of truth
you pull back the night
shine softly the moon
replant all that's good
in the poetry that's you...

Rain, Rain Come Again
Cindy Pagia

I found warmth
Under your raincoat.
Caught in the rainstorm
With just a light coat.

My heart was so near
to your beating heart.
And deep down I fear
flames were sparked.

With your arm around
Trying to protect me,
I'm losing my ground
To fly with you, please let me.

And once the rain stopped
You just walked away.
My heart was tied in a knot.
Didn't know what to say.

Except to hope and pray
This is not the end.
Before you go away.
Rain, rain please come again.

Perchance to Dream
Tom Cleary

The wand of bed seduces head to sleep
a comfy pillow, mattress lure us down.
An open invitation, stationed deep
within subconscious wishes where we drown
in wealth of dreams as hunger for the taste
of softly colored sounds, aromas blend
commingled loosely, flowing into space
where childlike wonder once more is our friend.
Now lost in fantasy, forever free
we flit in fields so lush upon our feet
not even birds or yellow bumblebee
can float as easy nor as fly so fleet.

But stinging horsefly buzzes near to harm
we swat away the ring of our alarm.

Alfie's Place
Becky Tee

Follow the path to the left
Where the wild garlic fitfully grows
And the cherry blossom dances
On the breeze, like pink snow

There you'll find the fallen oak
Its ear to the whispering stream
Where once we looked for pirates' gold
Beneath that balancing beam

And, on that crumbling wall,
You often sat and swung your feet
Grasses towering over you
Pink cheeked in the summer heat

If you look behind you
The fields have found their grace
Wildflowers gently weave and wave
You always loved this place

So when you are sad or desolate
Remember our woodland days
Reverie will bring you here
And console you in so many ways

Overlapping Moons
Scot A. Buffington

Lie me alone, a crestfallen shadow
past azimuth's point, no recourse again
expected to rate a short-termed fellow
reserved to cry amongst well-broken men.

Affection's heart so easy unmasked
though, perhaps it must have clearly seen
intentions, my minds-eye should have asked
if I stood before, amongst, or between.

A sweet ricochet, an opportune course
place card holder 'til better suit came
number to claim as a worn-for-worse
hating the sound, my own spoken name.

Wheels turn quick, in stasis abstaining
time charred candles, wicking too fast
this era waxed as another's was waning
overlapping moons, knights of your past.

No soft remorse in angels' wings pining
presence shall ebb, as the tide from your shore
another new moon, much brighter shining
than my cratered surface, overcast poor.

Sinking by fathoms, horizon distant
never forget that I once glowed your night
perhaps these forevers, another one's instants
groping in darkness for soul-freeing light.

Little Perishers

Ryan Morgan

The crows perch
On winter's edge,
Shadows that search
For the lingering dead.

Upon the gaunt tree
Flat-stares glower down
From a haunted canopy
That wears a crow crown.

Each bird a murderous regent
Presiding over its winter domain,
Alert with insidious intent,
Dire winged harbingers of pain.

The lords of carrion
Alight at the last draw of breath,
Their obsidian clarion
Cry as a herald for Death.

This is their season,
Between dim solstice and spring,
When tenacity weakens
And to the grim precipice we cling.

In the cold sky they wheel,
Flocked spirals of dark majesty.
Their doleful flying reel
Evokes the cycle of mortality.

They wear restraint
Like a raven raiment.
They will wait.
They are ever patient.

Even the Rain Conspires
Bern Fraley

It feeds and freezes,
cracking the streets
away from our feet.

Winter is changing tense;
even when they tell us this afternoon
is going to cough-up one more hairball of snow,
I can feel the softness of sleet coming.

When I look out at the landscape,
the cold rain is pinning everything in place;
the universe no longer rotates with ease,
there are no odors at zero degrees.

When
Lorna McLaren

When the day forgets to dawn
and the birds forget to sing
I'll hold my tears close to my heart
for they won't mean a thing.
When the moon forgets to rise
and the stars forget to shine
that will be my time to weep
for you'll be no longer mine.
When there is but nothingness
with the skies remaining grey
I'll close my eyes, offer a smile
and simply fade away.

Rebirth

Terry Bridges

The awakening soul
A burst chrysalis
Attempting flight
Hopelessly like this

Screaming in thick air
Germinating to light
Moonshine permeates
The onrushing night

Tempest and tragedy
Stirs in the breeze
Cracking with laughter
No others to please

Hardened to a point
Concentrated fire
Erupting splendour
Higher and higher

Majesty in travel
Fleeing through the years
Certainty a harbour
Amid floods of tears

Daytime hours recede
Welcome black deliverer
Space in the twilight
To comfort to treasure

The fulfilled heart expands
At no forfeit of cost
Centred in the spectrum
All misgivings lost

No fear but in care
Rejoicing with my friends
They are everywhere
Nothing ever truly ends

The Wood of Want

E.C. McCaffrey

She had become a shadow, barely there.
The winter of her days had worn her thin
Merely a whisper leaving her dry and bare.
With no one to wander into the depth within

The hue of youth now fades into a grey.
A waning light seen through the opaque lens.
Leaving a burden that feels more like decay.
As footprints drift into the way back when

There are no storms that carry passions breath.
No tumult winds that bring forth life again
A silent stale with air that tastes like death.
Where sorrow broke the pride that would not bend

Gone is the fruit that once hung from her limbs.
The green of youth that shaded passions burn.
Here lies the wood where winter has set in.
Whose brittle bark no longer dares to yearn.

Forgotten dreams are lonely homes to dwell.
Without the keys, they feel more like a cell.

The Whispering Crows
Dale Parsons

Darkness dour, dawns lonely hour
Visions come and then go
Swirling, circling, a carousel of birds
A cavorting murder of crows
Nattering, chattering, niggling notions
Conceptions of caution grow
Incessant Interfering, persevering
Penetration when eyes close
Feathered fiends infiltrating dreams
Words of warning they bestow
Uttering, muttering of what's to come
A morbid undertow
Tidings tearing through a tired mind
Bound by the eyes of the crows

A New 'Now' at the End of the Poem
Jessica Ferreira Coury Magalhães

Clutching my years hard in my closed fists
Afraid they'll roll away and say goodbye.

Stretching the days and the nights
Like a rubber band that, at the same time,
Is accommodating, but will hold me tight.

I'm greedy with the minutes and the hours
Making a point to fill them up equal parts
With daydream and a concrete design
To treasure, marvel, wonder, delight.

All this is on my schedule for now
Which is already gone by as I write.
A new 'now' begins at the next line:
Over-fixate on the fact that I walk among the living
Now that I finally like my life.

blink

Matt Elmore

I'm no puppet on some stage
for strange plays and time to waste
not my taste being hasty and chased
when too much pressure from my peers
make me blink then disappear

because I'm human I make mistakes
cracks of ice leak in lakes from my face
deep run rakes in soft soil left to forsake
as too much pressure from my peers
makes me sink then disappear

profound hounds give and take
amend contend; cut and paste
blunders in slumbers unseen, now awake!
when too much pressure from my peers
make me blink then disappear

Name it to Tame it

Dara C. Vazquez

They whimpered, the untamed
babes, coming to him being unnamed.
Crawling bellies naked across the floors
Scribbled writings upon walls and doors.
Uncivilized, bare, without titled care
unabashed findings in the invisible lair.
Precious stories, orally told, with
no way to seek beyond memory to hold.
To be set upon a stage
immortalized upon a page
a rebellious and wild
neglected, unadorned child.
And he tamed them, each one and the same.
For each the first line, he clothed them in their name.

When Shall the World in Splendour Rise

Valerie Dohren

When shall the world in splendour rise
To touch those sweet empyreal skies
Above all things in shadows cast
As captured there through years long passed

And when shall the world with eyes that see
Unite as one, in harmony,
To take his neighbour for his friend
All strife and warfare so to end

When shall the world with hearts that care
Provide for all, its wealth to share,
None to suffer deprivation
Plentiful for every nation

And when shall the world with love imbued
Be no more sad, no more subdued,
Let happiness surround each day
All sorrow thus to fade away

O when shall the world in full rejoice
E`er speak out loud with equal voice
Dance in peace and touch the flowers
To celebrate this world of ours

I Think Not
Shirley Rose

I don't know if she deep dives
To where the oysters are
In order to harvest their pearls
Or whether she is the oyster herself
Slowly forming her own precious gems

I don't know if she gathers the colors
To paint the sky its array of sunrise hues
That of orange and yellow, pink and coral, turquoise blues
Wielding brush and rag to drip and drag stripes across the dawn...

Or if she's Dawn herself, rising from her darkened bed of night
Upon stretching and yawning perhaps her very breath
Becomes the morning rays...

I don't know if she walks among the flowers and trees
Plucking pods ripe with seeds,
gently opening them within their time
Planting them in ground she has freshly primed...
Or maybe *she* is the fertile soil, the very bed that new life needs...

Perhaps she is the seed, pod, acorn, cone, weed, grasses...

I know not if the stars await her command to blow their gasses
Causing the nuclear fusion needed to start their very life
Or if, in searching for her, they cause such internal pressure and
Extreme gravity as to become her subjects, shining hard and
bright...

Perhaps she's the very essence of existence at a molecular level
And what we see of the beings we know — animal, mineral, gas —
Oyster, pearl, sun and star, green growth, the universe — and us —
Are merely coincidental happenstance of ironic incident...

But I think not

Let Us Drink Tea

Sarah Joy Holden

Pop a bag into a porcelain pot
Pour in water make sure it's hot
Stir it round, right then stir left
Let it brew until it looks right

A brew for one, a brew for a few
There's a brew for a poetry crew
My Father tells me too let it stew
My Mother say let the tea brew

Ah, what fine brew or two that was
A heavenly beverage to touch my lips
Tea's the answer when the world's at odds
With all it different scents and flavours

Tea and poetry is my daily prescription
Without which, I cannot possibly function
To family 'n' friends my love of tea is known
No reason for the 'tea or coffee' question

I drink my brew, as I always do
I drink cup one and then another two
It's caffeine boast makes me up and go
For a cup of tea, I can never say no

I Found Life

Becky Tee

I found life
In that little flower
And forgiveness
In the chime of the hour

I found freedom
I saw it in his eyes
And liberty
In the absence of disguise

I found nostalgia
In the scent of the trees
And an enchanting tale
In his muddy knees

I found a story
In the knots in her hair
And secrets
In the midnight air

I found a whisper
In the fitful breeze
And distraction
In the gossiping leaves

I found beauty
In the starlit sky
And love
In the canine's eye

I found happiness
When my soul began to see
The very moment
In front of me

When I See the Light
of Sunshine Once Again

Martin Gedge

Surrounded by the shadows
that are closing in on me
cracking through the surface
of the walls I built for thee
In tears that drown my sorrows
sure to soak of my regret
playing on my memories
letting know I can't forget
the pain so pure of purpose
on the sores that break my heart
I watch as life goes passing
while I'm grasping for a spark
to give me all the meaning
and the strength to carry on
In air of every prayer
to feel the care before I'm gone
to know that tried and true
my love for you will hold a flame
to hear of every whisper
on the lips that winds my name
you see in portrait pictures
with a smile to wear my face
of warmth and gentle comfort
in the arms of saving grace
the past to last within the mind
of time and changing days
on nights of many moons to bloom
in rooms where gardens graze
that in my fields to roam
you welcome home a fathers son
as free as any soul to fly
the sky who wants to run…

Close to Nature
Yusuf M. Khalid

Close to nature
in the countryside
humid and windless
after the rain
The fireflies
in the dark
looked like stars
within reach

With a ladle
yellowish brown
I drank some milk
in a calabash
One would think
they forged of gold
but not the wild
trailing gourd

I lay down
on a raffia mat
a handicraft
so sublime
a full circle
of hued weave
a void-less halo
of rainbow

To and fro
waved a hand fan
made of the feathers
of a peacock
ocellated
green and blue
akin to half Earth
viewed on moon

The Stars Blink

J.T. Caine

The stars blink
Like the neurons in my brain
Distant and adrift
Fires burning in refrain

When you found me
Just a dog along the highway
Trusting foolishly
All the dangers headed my way

My universe expands
But still I remain the same
Falling into cracks
Microscopic, I proclaim

Sometimes the darkness
Seems to extinguish all the light
A harbinger of times
When the days won't chase the night

Where do they run to
These kaleidoscopic fever dreams
When I succumb to
Wakefulness and all her schemes

Supernaught

Ronnie Tucker

In flights of angels
Wrapped in bands of gold
Shifting in changes
No longer seeing through the eyes of a child
With a ghost in the pocket

Held in prisms of a locket
Time is only a reflection left to dream
Lost in a state of confusion
A smile in decay
So beautiful, so dangerous

In fluttering of blankets of wings
Stir restless angels
As innumerable numbers are tossed like dice
Burning in effigies with faces so familiar
Bitter is the serpents of the tongue

In rituals start the dance
So ecstatic, thaumaturgy hath been woven
Underneath the Styx to ply the tricks
In the order, metamorphosis to creepy crawl
Unto eyes the color runs

Who is this God I wear on my shoulders?
Does he mock to destroy?
In heaven there's no answer
Only to conform
And bend in shape

Ornaments divine
Unto arts so sublime
Mystical lips purified
Beneath their crooked smiles

The ancient tongues of angels have no reply

Strange exists to existence
Yes we be damned fools
To open this door
And tread this madness
And bleed like holy water

The kiss is sweet sorrow
As we hide ourselves in plain sight
Throwing stones to the center
A cosmic game well played
No the visions are dead now

Isolation is but loneliness
Desolation is but the void to despair
Come as you are
Translucent and transparent
Some dusky stranger heaven sent

Just one look
And I know it probably will
Just one wink and I know it will
The heart is but a hollow dream
So Infinite in its beating illusion

Segue into sequences
Ashes to colored reality
Natural is the order to chaos
Illuminating the angelic refrains
Woven in their wings sustained

Opaque to all points of view
Drunken from a cup of heavens dew
So deep is the eternal flame that burns
Hidden behind a wall of confusion
Sweet surrender to the nocturnal supernaught

Stone Cold in Winter

Graeme Stokes

The hustling street traffic just contradicts,
as I survey your dark lonely space
The emptiness can only fill, when harsh time resists,
the clock hand's languorous pace

A futile ray of sun greets your vacant spot,
bemused at the salient absence
Beats a hasty retreat, to the clouds in deep thought,
shaken by the daily imbalance

Memories still chatter in the shop window glass,
a backlog of tales to spill
My grieving reflection tunes into the past,
recollections cut raw and fresh still!

Your buoyant essence wafts in the teasing wind,
the tangible scent of perfume
The delusory promise is quickly rescinded,
retreating in vacuous plumes

Interlopers occupy the scene of the crime,
a dagger thrust into my heart
Sharp laughter, stings like a bullet ant's ire,
my symmetry on an alien march

Hope is dashed to the insipid lips,
crushed under reality's roll
Peace of mind draining in torturous drips,
that transmit to my drowning soul

Resistance bleeds on the dispassionate floor,
existence limps on with sharp splinters
My face stares at your space with a freezing core,
stone cold features in my dead of winter!

Embraced
Rohan Primrose

Walking bare foot along a foreign shore
Salt drying on my brow
wet from a Hawaiian tide
Mind swings to larger thoughts small

Enriched by paternal joy
An adventure shared and taken to task
The smile in the grind of an upstream valley
to a waterfall of magnificence

The expression of delight and wonder
a distant sunset over a distant horizon
13748 feet of vantage
The glint in your eye
Not wanting an end.

Feelings of nervousness
Pensive danger between the ears ignored.
But the courage to leap into dark waters
The prize of natures close encounter.

A new awakening of maturing mind
Of one's own spirit crafted not created
An inner drive of the rights and wrongs
Of rites of passage earned not given.

Embracing a world of adventure
As your world opens before my eyes.

Little by Little

John Jolam

seen it all, and more;
how they took us out.
heart from their hearts
talks whispers at our backs
and surely life's a thing, or two
and span has gone on full regret.
when time to sleeps it does
and sleep without dreams
or dreams would cross
and dress from each are torn
(nothing gathers like moss)
in time there's to remember
and all what was taught.
where it had a mind of its own,
the fresh was eaten hard
boneless in ointment dis-ease.
where inside was its mind
outside was its stories; and
little by little, something grew.
little, getting small and smaller.

About Wheelsong Books

Wheelsong Books is an independent poetry publishing
company based in the ocean city of Plymouth,
on the beautiful Southwest coast of England.
Established by poet Steve Wheeler in 2019,
the company aims to promote previously unheard voices
and encourage new talent in poetry. Wheelsong is also
the home of the Absolutely Poetry anthology series,
featuring previously unpublished and emerging poets
from around the globe.

Wheelsong has more poetry publications in the pipeline!
You can read more about Wheelsong Books and its growing
stable of exciting new and emerging poets on the
Wheelsong Books website at: wheelsong.co.uk

Wheelsong publication list

- Ellipsis (2020) by Steve Wheeler
- Inspirations (2020) by Kenneth Wheeler
- Sacred (2020) by Steve Wheeler
- Living by Faith (2020) by Kenneth Wheeler
- Urban Voices (2020) by Steve Wheeler
- Small Lights Burning (2021) by Steve Wheeler
- My Little Eye (2021) by Steve Wheeler
- Ascent (2021) by Steve Wheeler
- Dance of the Metaphors (2021) by Rafik Romdhani
- Into the Grey (2021) by Brandon Adam Haven
- RITE (2021) by Steve Wheeler
- Absolutely Poetry Anthology 1 (2021) by various
- Absolutely Poetry Anthology 2 (2022) by various
- War Child (2022) by Steve Wheeler
- Hoyden's Trove (2022) by Jane Newberry
- Shocks and Stares (2022) by Steve Wheeler
- Autumn Shedding (2022) by Christian Ryan Pike
- Cobalt Skies (2022) by Charlene Phare
- Wheelsong Poetry Anthology 1 (2022) by various
- Rough Roads (2022) by Rafik Romdhani
- Symphoniya de Toska: Book One (2023) by Marten Hoyle
- Vapour of the Mind (2023) by Rafik Romdhani
- Nocturne (2023) by Steve Wheeler
- Symphoniya de Toska: Book Two (2023) by Marten Hoyle
- Wheelsong Poetry Anthology 2 (2023) by various
- Constellation Road (2023) by Matthew Elmore
- Beyond the Pyre (2023) by Imelda Zapata Garcia
- Symphoniya de Toska: Book Three (2023) by Marten Hoyle
- Wheelsong Poetry Anthology 3 (2023) by various
- This Broken House (2023) by Brandon Adam Haven
- All the Best (2024) by Steve Wheeler

All titles are available for purchase in paperback, and Kindle editions and some in hardcover on Amazon.com or direct from the publisher at: wheelsong.co.uk

Printed in Great Britain
by Amazon

37661672R00167